JOEL DEWBERRY'S
sewn
SPACES

JOEL DEWBERRY'S
sewn
SPACES

joel dewberry

Krause Publications
CINCINNATI, OHIO

www.fwmedia.com.

14   13   12   11   10   5   4   3   2   1

Distributed in Canada by Fraser Direct
100 Armstrong Avenue
Georgetown, ON, Canada L7G 5S4
Tel: (905) 877-4411

Distributed in the U.K. and Europe by David & Charles
Brunel House, Newton Abbot, Devon, TQ12 4PU,
England
Tel: (+44) 1626 323200, Fax: (+44) 1626 323319
Email: postmaster@davidandcharles.co.uk

Distributed in Australia by Capricorn Link
P.O. Box 704, S. Windsor NSW, 2756 Australia
Tel: (02) 4577-3555

Library of Congress Cataloging in Publication Data
Dewberry, Joel.
  Joel Dewberry's sewn spaces / Joel Dewberry. -- 1st ed.
     p. cm.
  Includes index.
  ISBN-13: 978-0-89689-924-7 (pbk. : alk. paper)
  ISBN-10: 0-89689-924-1 (pbk. : alk. paper)
  1. Textile crafts. I. Title. II. Title: Sewn spaces.
  TT699.D493 2010
  746--dc22
                          2009048737

Edited by Vanessa Lyman
Designed by Michelle Thompson
Production coordinated by Matt Wagner and
Greg Nock
Photography by Ric Deliantoni
Photography styled by Nora Martini and
Megan Strasser

About the Author

Joel Dewberry brings a fresh, modern sensibility to design. After acquiring more than 10 years of brand development experience in a wide variety of industries, including the home and textile market, Joel launched his own textiles brand, Joel Dewberry Eclectic Modern, in May 2007. To see his fabric collections and locate a retailer, visit his website at www.joeldewberry.com.

Even more than being a designer, the role he is most passionate about is that as a husband and father. With four children, he and his wife have their hands full.

METRIC CONVERSION CHART

To convert	to	multiply by
Inches	Centimeters	2.54
Centimeters	Inches	0.4
Feet	Centimeters	30.5
Centimeters	Feet	0.03
Yards	Meters	0.9
Meters	Yards	1.1

Acknowledgments

Special thanks to the following individuals: My editor, Vanessa Lyman, for her patience and unwavering focus that kept us on track throughout the process. Jay Staten and Jamie Markle for having the confidence in our concept and giving us the opportunity to share our ideas with so many. Michelle Thompson, a brilliant book designer, who captured the spirit of my style throughout these pages. For the amazing folks at Westminster Fibers/FreeSpirit Fabrics who supplied the fabric and who continue to translate my designs and vision into something tangible. For my sister-in-law Carly Lowry, whose sewing expertise and love for fabric were valuable assets in completing all of the sewing projects. Finally, I give my love and appreciation for my mother Donna Dewberry, an amazing woman with an endless passion for cultivating her talents and inspiring me to follow.

Many thanks to everyone who contributed to this book, especially to all those who share my love for fabric.

Dedication

This book is dedicated to my wife Laurie as she is my unending source of inspiration and motivation. Without her support and tireless effort designing, sewing, and writing for this book, I would have not completed this work.

contents

My passion for fabric design stems from the warmth, texture and color it offers to so many aspects of our lives. Fabric is the perfect medium for making a statement of personal expression, invigorating a room in your home with the right amount of texture and pattern or adding comfortable warmth to a handmade quilt.

When designing my fabric collections, I incorporate design elements from a mixture of design styles, and thus felt it most appropriate to describe the style of these collections as Eclectic Modern. Eclectic Modern is simply another way of describing the unexpected harmony that can exist between modern design and vintage charm. This approach to design is meant to reinvigorate something classic, such as an antique piece of furniture or traditional quilt design, with fresh and modern design sensibilities. Imagine a discarded antique chair given new life by a fresh coat of paint in a bold and memorable color and then upholstered with an equally distinctive piece of fabric.

It is a style that resonates with me because it encourages no boundaries; no preconceived notions of which design styles are acceptable to be blended together. Eclectic Modern style encourages an individual to simply embrace what they believe to be lovely and inspiring and allows their imagination to weave the thread that brings all of the elements into harmony. Sometimes it is color, other times it is a pattern or texture. Regardless, there is no right or wrong, just an opportunity to surround yourself with the things you enjoy the most. You will see that the projects in this book also reflect my love for a variety of styles.

The inspiration for the name of this book comes from my desire to show how fabric can enhance or even transform any of the living spaces you find yourself in each day. My intent is to show simple ways in which a person who has a passion for fabric and sewing can infuse their personality into the world around them and to inspire others by the spaces they create. There is an unrivaled satisfaction that comes from truly defining a space that captures your individuality, and I hope the projects presented in the pages ahead will give you the confidence to create your own "sewn space."

—— *Joel Dewberry*

notions and other materials

Part of the fun in starting a new project is the opportunity to collect new tools and supplies. Though all the fabrics and supplies you'll need for each project are listed at the beginning of that project, here is a comprehensive list of supplies used in this book.

Basics
Fabric
Coordinating thread
Sewing machine
Seam ripper
Iron
Ironing board or pressing pad
Scissors
Needles

Cutting Supplies
Scissors
Cutting mat
Rotary cutter
Stencil cutter
Box cutter
Craft blade

Stuffing
Low-loft batting
Foam pillow form
Light-weight batting
Polyester fiberfill
½"-thick bonded polyester batting

Adhesives
Spray adhesive
Quick-setting craft glue
Masking tape

Interfacing
Fusible interfacing
Double-sided fusible interfacing
Fusible backing

Marking Tools
Marking pen
Graphite paper
Chalk pencil or fabric marker
Fabric pencil
Pencil
Dressmaker pencil
Carbon transfer paper
Bone folder / scoring tool

Pins and Needles
Upholstery tacks
Straight pins
Staple gun and staples
Embroidery needle(s) (various sizes)
Hand sewing needle(s) (various sizes)
Sewing machine needle(s) (various sizes)
Safety pin

Measuring Tools
Ruler
Measuring tape
Yardstick

Embellishment Tools
Beads
Cording
Ribbon (grosgrain)
Embroidery floss

Other supplies
Cardstock
½"-wide elastic
11" × 17" clear transparency (for screen printing)
8" × 10" piece of glass
Sponge or craft paint roller
1¾" metal button
Button covering kit
1 sew-on snap
12" wooden dowels
Floral tape
Contact paper
Glass etching cream
Camera
Pliers
Staple gun and staples
Hammer
Sandpaper
Paintbrush
Exterior latex satin paint
Primer
Large, papier mâché letter
Decoupage medium
15" embroidery hoop
Plastic drywall corner bead
1" craft brush
Acrylic paint
Fishing line
Drapery clips
Mat board

machine stitches

Most of the machine stitching in these projects will be straight stitch or zigzag. Whether you're sewing with a no-frills sewing machine, or the latest computerized model, follow these basic machine-sewing rules: Choose a needle that is appropriate for the weight of the fabric and tightly insert it into your machine. Select a presser foot that is appropriate to the task. Wind your bobbin and thread your machine with the same thread. Select the stitch setting on your machine, then slide a scrap of fabric under the presser foot and sew some sample stitches. Adjust the stitch length until you determine the stitch length and width you want.

When sewing, keep the fabric straight by guiding it with your fingers. Follow the ruler marking to give your sewn project an even seam allowance.

Straight Stitch

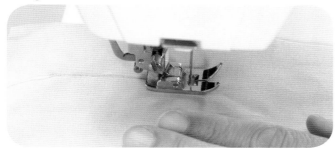

1 Select the straight stitch setting and desired stitch length. Lower the presser foot and begin sewing by pressing the peddle. Backstitch a few stitches at the beginning to secure stitching.

2 Continue sewing until you've reached the end. Backstitch a few stitches. Lift the presser foot, and clip the threads to remove the fabric.

Zig Zag Stitch

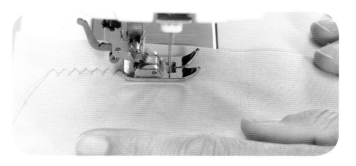

1 Select the zigzag stitch setting and desired stitch length. Lower the presser foot and begin sewing by pressing the peddle.

For an appliqué stitch, choose a low stitch width and a short stitch length.

2 Continue sewing until you've reached the end, and backstitch a few stitches. Lift the presser foot, and clip the threads to remove the fabric.

backstitch

The backstitch is an easy stitch often used for outlining. Most commonly three strands of floss are used for this stitch, but you can use more or less depending on the look you want.

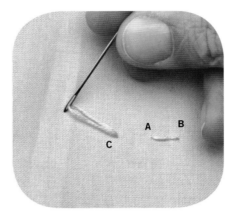

1 You will be working from right to left. Bring the thread to the right side of the fabric, about one stitch-length from the right end of the line you will be stitching (A).

Move your needle one stitch-length (length determined by you) to the right of where your floss emerged (B) and push it back down to the wrong side.

2 Bring your needle back through to the right side one stitch-length to the left of where the first stitch began (C).

3 Then, take your needle back through the fabric to the wrong side, right next to where your first stitch began (D).

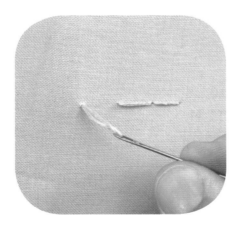

4 Continue along your line, repeating steps 1 through 3.

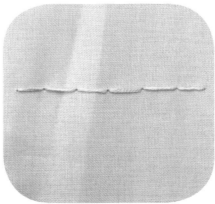

5 When you take the last stitch to the wrong side, tie a knot.

satin stitch

The satin stitch is used to fill in a defined shape. Most commonly three strands of floss are used for this stitch, but you can use more or less depending on the look you want.

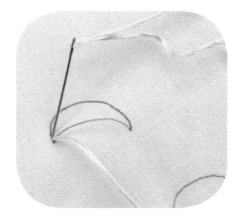

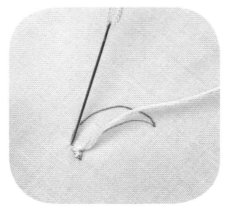

1 Insert your needle from the wrong side of the fabric to the right side at the left corner of your design. Insert the needle from the right to wrong side at the opposite edge of the design as shown.

2 Bring the needle from the wrong side to the right side, right next to where your first stitch started. Pull the floss taut so that it lies flat.

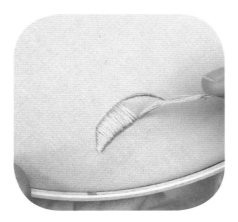

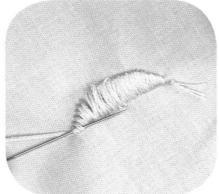

3 Continue stitching along the shape of the design following steps 1 and 2, placing the stitches close together, until the shape is filled.

4 Once the shape is complete, bring the needle through to the wrong side of the fabric. Hide the floss tail by weaving it under the stitches and tie a knot.

split stitch

The split stitch is also a useful stitch for outlining shapes or for flower stems. This stitch works best with an even number of floss strands. Four strands are most commonly used.

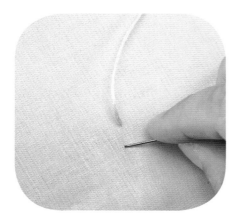 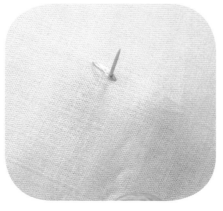 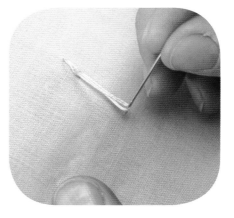

1 Thread the needle with 2 or 4 strands of floss. Bring the needle to the right side of the fabric, pull it through, then insert the needle from the right to the wrong side about ⅛" to ¼" away. Pull the floss taut.

2 Bring the needle up through the center of the first stitch, splitting the floss with the needle.

3 Pull the floss through to the right side to complete the first stitch. To begin the second stitch, insert the needle from the right to wrong side about ⅛" to ¼" away and pull floss taut.

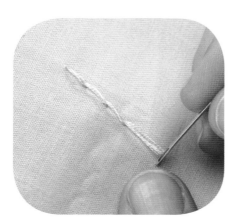 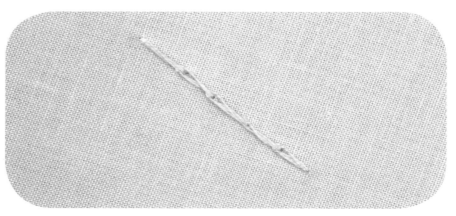

4 Continue working the stitches in the same manner along a line.

5 When you've reached the end of the line, pull the floss to the wrong side and tie a knot.

lazy daisy stitch

The lazy daisy stitch is a useful stitch for creating leaves or flower petals. For best results, use three strands of floss.

1 Using a fabric marker, draw a five-petaled design on the right side of the fabric. Bring the needle through to the right side of the fabric at the bottom of one petal.

2 Following the left edge of the petal design, loop the floss around the petal shape, and insert the needle from the right side to the wrong side, right next to where the floss first emerged.

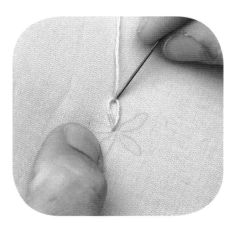

3 Bring the needle from the wrong side to the right side at the tip of the flower petal. Pull the floss through, then loop it over the tip of the petal, from the right to wrong side, to anchor the petal in place.

4 Repeat steps 1-3 to complete the other petals, then bring the needle to the wrong side and tie a knot.

blanket stitch

The blanket stitch is typically used along the fabric edge. Most commonly three strands of floss are used for this stitch, but you can use more or less depending on the look you want.

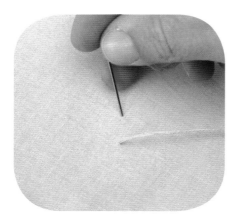

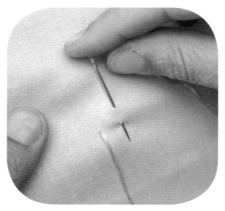

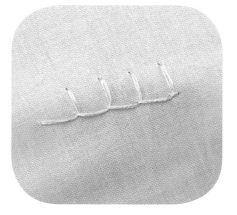

1 Bring your needle through to the right side of the fabric. Position the needle about ¼" away, above and to the right.

2 Bring the needle back through to the right side, as shown, about ¼" to the right of where the needle first emerged.

3 Before pulling the needle all the way through, tuck the loose floss under the needle point.

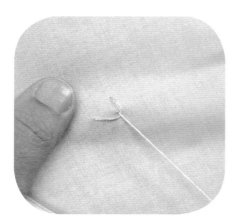

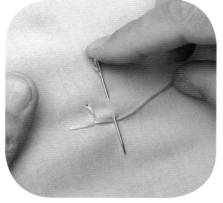

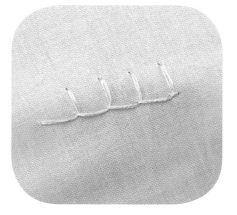

4 Pull the needle through, forming a backward L-shaped stitch.

5 Bring the needle over about ¼" away, above and to the right. Insert the needle partway about ¼" to the right side of the previous stitch. Tuck the loose floss under the needle point, then pull it all the way though.

6 Repeat steps 1-5 until you've reached the end of your design. Each new stitch will secure the loop of the previous stitch. To finish, take a small stitch to the wrong side and tie a knot.

stem stitch

The stem stitch is primarily used for outlining and flower stems. Most commonly three strands of floss are used for this stitch, but you can use more or less depending on the look you want.

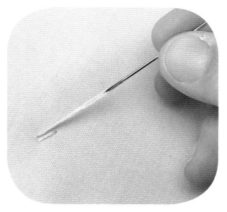

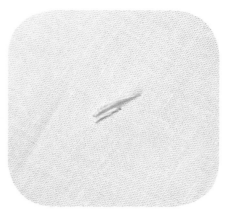

1 Bring the thread to the right side of the fabric at the left edge of your line. Insert the needle to the right about ¼" and push through to the wrong side. (Be sure to keep the thread below the needle as you push it through.)

2 Bring the needle back through to the right side just above where the first stitch started. Pull the floss through until the first stitch lies flat. Begin your next stitch.

3 Insert the needle (from the right side to the wrong side) to the right, veering down a bit so the needle is inserted along the same line as the first stitch.

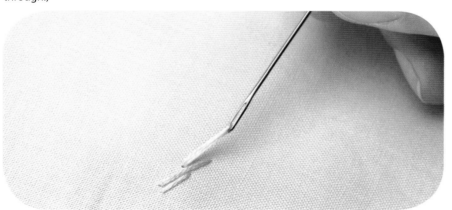

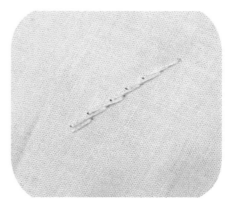

4 Repeat steps 1-3. Your first stitch will be the shortest; the remaining stitches will be twice its length. Keep the tension even and the remaining stitches the same length. Stitches that are close together make a tight line. Those that are farther away make a looser line.

5 When you are finished, bring the needle to the wrong side and tie a knot.

french knot

The French knot is used for creating small circles and fine details in embroidery designs. The more strands of floss you use, the larger the knot.

1 Thread your needle with 3 strands of floss and knot the end. Bring the needle through from the wrong side of the fabric to the right side of the fabric.

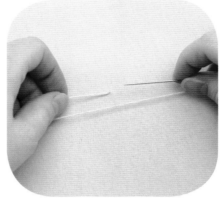

2 Hold the floss firmly between your left index finger and thumb, pulling it taut and away from where it emerged.

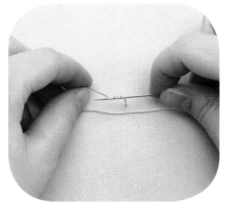

3 With your left hand, wrap the floss around the needle two or three times. (The more loops, the larger the knot will be.)

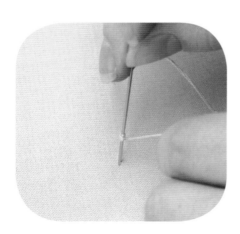

4 Insert the needle into the fabric from the right side to the wrong side right next to where it first emerged, holding the floss taut with your left hand.

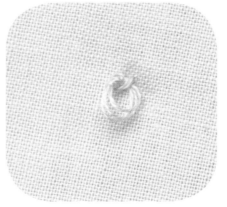

5 Pull the needle all the way through to the wrong side. The floss on the front side will form loops that will grow smaller as you pull the floss taut.

6 When the floss is pulled taut, the final French knot should lay relatively flat against the fabric. Secure with a knot on the wrong side

buttonholes

Buttonholes are most generally used for exactly what the name suggests, but several projects in this book utilize the buttonhole for the openings to a drawstring casing. The bound opening allows the drawstring to be easily pulled without fraying the opening.

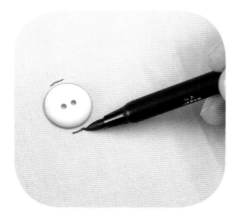

1 Measure and mark the placement of the buttonhole on your fabric with a fabric marker.

2 For added reinforcement, iron a piece of fusible interfacing to the wrong side of the fabric where your buttonhole will go.

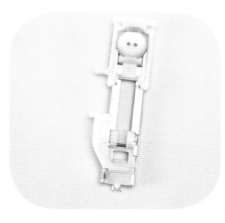

3 Place a button in the machine's buttonhole foot to establish the buttonhole length. (Or set the buttonhole length on your machine or buttonhole foot.)

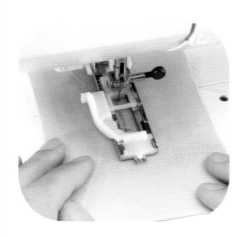

4 Attach the buttonhole foot to the machine and sew the buttonhole following your machine's instruction manual for stitching buttonholes.

5 Once the stitching is complete, cut the thread, pull the fabric out of the machine and use a seam ripper to cut a slit inside the stitching to open the buttonhole.

6 Trim any loose strings or frayed edges from the buttonhole.

button covering

Fabric-covered buttons give a project a nice finished look and can easily be made with a store-bought kit.

1 Cut a circle from a fabric scrap about ⅝" larger than the button form.

2 Lay the fabric circle right-side-down over the button-making kit cylinder.

3 Push the top of the button into the cylinder (over the fabric) and wrap the fabric over the edge of the button top.

4 Push the back of the button into the cylinder, making sure to catch all of the fabric and fabric edges tightly.

5 Secure the button back by pushing down firmly with the plastic finishing piece.

6 Remove the finished, fabric-covered button from the cylinder.

dart

Darts are stitched V-shapes used to shape fabric by making it less full at the wide end of the dart, while keep it full at the point of the dart.

1 Transfer the dart markings to the *wrong* side of the fabric using a straightedge and a fabric marker.

2 With *right* sides facing, fold the dart in half lengthwise. Make sure the fold comes to a point at the small circle at the bottom of the dart.

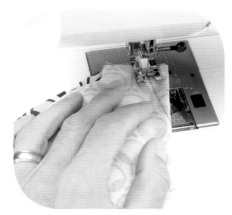

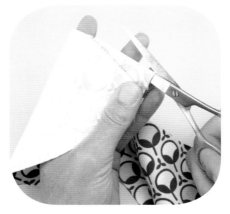

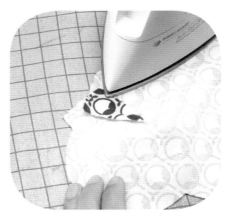

3 Sew along the line of the dart from the circle at the top to the circle at the bottom, backstitching at the beginning and end of the dart.

4 Cut the dart open along the fold.

5 Press the dart open.

piping

Piping is fabric-covered cording used for decorative edging on a project. Here we are inserting piping around the outside edges of the pillow cover.

1 Cut cording to desired length. Cut a 1"-wide strip of fabric about 1" longer than the piece of cording. Lay the fabric strip right-side-down and place the cording in the center.

2 Fold the fabric in half over the cording and pin in place. Using a zipper foot, sew through both fabric layers. This is your piping.

3 Sandwich the piping between the *right* sides of the pillow cover front and back, matching all raw edges; pin in place.

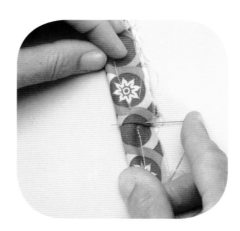

4 Using a zipper foot, sew all the fabric layers together along the edge of the cording. Sew all four sides, but leave a 4-6" opening on one side unsewn.

5 When you are about 4" from the end of the piping, remove this pillow cover from the sewing machine. Fold over the raw edge of piping about ¼".

6 Lay the folded edge over the raw edge of the other end of the piping. Sew in place. Turn the pillow cover right-side-out, stuff the pillow and use the zipper foot to sew closed.

appliqué

Appliqué is a technique used for sewing a piece of fabric onto another with either a machine appliqué stitch or machine satin stitch. Typically a contrasting fabric is used so the appliqué piece is easily visible on the project.

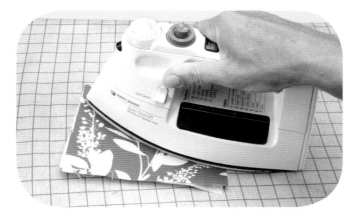

1 Cut a piece of fabric that is at least ¼" larger than the appliqué design. Iron a piece of double-sided fusible interfacing to the wrong side of the fabric piece.

2 Pin or trace your design to the right side of the fabric. Cut out the design.

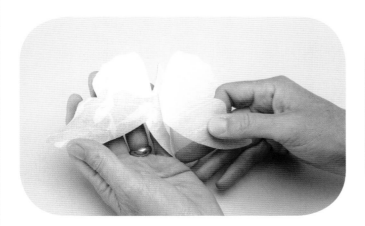

3 Peel the paper backing from the fusible interfacing and fuse the design onto the project at the desired location.

4 Select the appliqué stitch on your machine (or use a tight zigzag or satin stitch), then stitch around the edge of your appliqué design through all the layers.

23

glass etching

Glass etching is a quick way to achieve a sophisticated and permanent design embellishment on glass. All the materials you'll need are available online or at your local craft store; just be sure to follow the manufacturer's directions for using them.

1 Cut a piece of contact paper slightly larger than the glass you will be etching (leave about ½" margin all the way around).

2 To apply the contact paper, peel off the backing, lay the contact paper sticky-side-up on your work surface, and then lay the glass over the contact paper.

3 Turn the glass facedown and remove any air bubbles in the contact paper by pushing them to the edges. Trim excess contact paper along the edge of the glass.

4 Select a silhouetted design. Position graphite paper underneath the printed design and on top of the contact paper

5 Transfer the design to the contact paper by tracing the shapes with a pen or pencil.

6 Using a craft blade, cut along the outside edge of the design. Peel off the designs revealing exposed glass in those areas.

7 Apply the glass etching cream to the cut out areas following the manufacturer's instructions.

8 When the etching cream has been rinsed off, peel off the contact paper to reveal the etchings.

at play

The spaces we find ourselves in each day include more than just the permanent rooms in our home. Sometimes the spaces that help us find meaning in our lives or help us to relax and rejuvenate our spirits are spaces outside the home or spaces that travel with us. While we may share these spaces with many other people, we can still bring our own individuality into the space.

Think about the places where you develop your talents or practice your hobbies or celebrate important moments. Perhaps one of the projects featured in this section will enhance one of your playful spaces. Take your personality with you to the farmer's market with an oversized tote, or send a bouquet of fabric roses to a friend who will have a permanent reminder of your concern for them. Life is more than just work and routine; we have to find those moments and places that help us renew our spirits.

hello
CARD

Step 1. Cut cardstock.
    a. Cut out a 10" × 6 ½" piece of cardstock. Fold it in half to 5" × 6½".

    b. Cut a 6½" × 5" piece of cardstock (to cover the inside front panel of the card).

Step 2. Trace bird and cut out.
    a. Trace the bird pattern in the center of the card's front panel.

    b. Cut along the traced lines with a craft knife.

    c. Cut the fabric and the batting to fit behind the bird opening.

    d. Sandwich the fabric between the batting and the cut-out front panel so that the fabric appears right-side-up through the cut-out.

    e. Machine sew a straight stitch about ⅛" from the edge of the bird, making sure to catch the fabric and batting within the stitch.

Step 3. Finish card.
    a. Write the word "Hello" onto the front of the card.

    b. Thread a needle with two strands of embroidery floss and backstitch (see page 12) over the writing through all the layers.

    c. Spray adhesive on the back of the small piece of cardstock from step 1b, then glue it to the inside of the card's front panel to cover the fabric and batting.

MATERIALS LIST

fabric
5" × 5½" scrap of lightweight fabric

other supplies
Cardstock

Coordinating thread

Craft knife

Cutting mat

Embroidery floss

Embroidery needle with small eye

Pencil

Scissors

Small piece of low-loft batting

Spray adhesive

Sewing machine

Bird pattern (page 120)

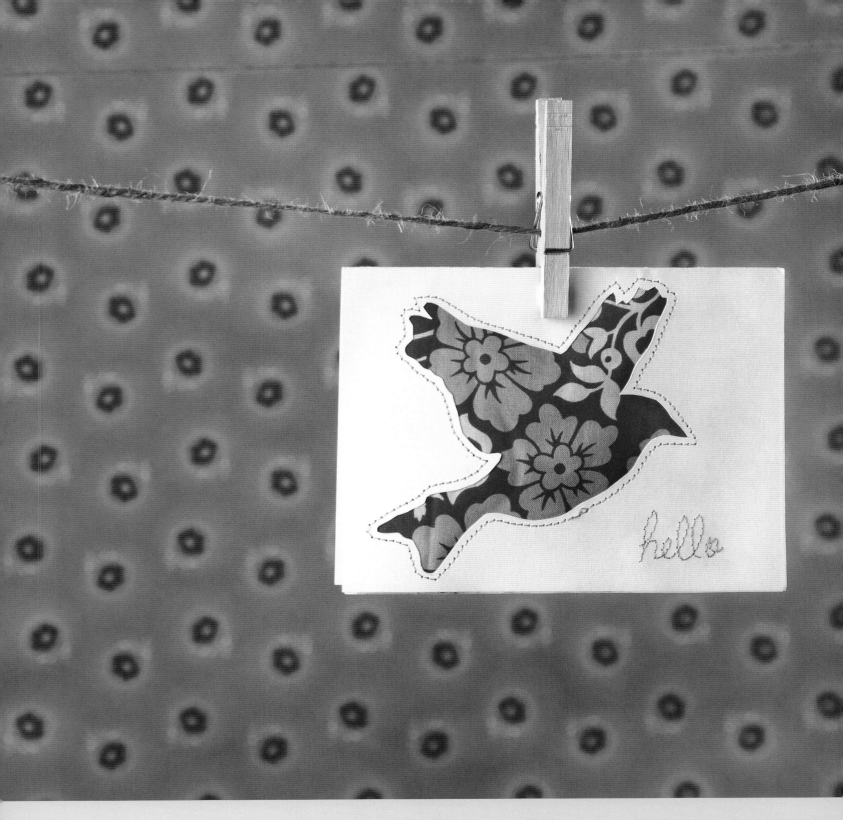

hello

thank you
CARD

Step 1. Cut cardstock pieces.

    a. Cut two 4½" × 11" pieces of cardstock.

Step 2. Cut out butterfly and finish card.

    a. Iron a piece of fusible interfacing to the *wrong* side of the small fabric scrap (3" × 3").

    b. Trace the butterfly onto the interfacing side of the fabric and cut it out.

    c. Using spray adhesive, affix the larger scrap of fabric to the bottom center of one of the cardstock pieces (about ¼" from the bottom and side edges), leaving 6½" of blank card stock above the fabric.

    d. Machine sew a straight stitch about ¼" inch from the raw edges of the fabric.

    e. Thread an embroidery needle with two strands of embroidery floss and sew the butterfly and antennae to the card with a backstitch (see page 12).

    f. Using a backstitch, hand sew the words "Thank you" to the *right* side of the bottom of the unused piece of cardstock.

    g. Affix the *wrong* sides of the two cardstock pieces together using spray adhesive. Fold the card over so that the words "Thank you" show below the fabric panel.

MATERIALS LIST

fabric

4¼" × 4½" scrap of lightweight fabric

3" × 3" scrap of coordinating fabric for butterfly

3" × 3" piece of fusible interfacing

other supplies

Cardstock

Craft knife

Cutting mat

Embroidery floss

Embroidery needle with small eye

Iron & ironing board

Pencil

Scissors

Sewing machine

Sewing thread in coordinating color

Spray adhesive

Butterfly pattern (page 120)

fabric
ROSES

Step 1. Cut fabric pieces and sew.

a. Cut out one 4¾" × 33" piece from fabrics A and fabric B, and one 12" length of grosgrain ribbon for each flower.

b. With *right* sides facing, sew the A and B pieces along one long edge. Press the seam open.

c. Fold the sewn fabric with *right* sides together again. Place the scallop pattern with the pattern's straightedge at the fabric seam/fold line and the scalloped edges ¼" from the raw edges of the fabric. Using a fabric pencil, trace the scallop design down the entire length of the fabric.

d. Machine stitch along the scallop line and the left edge. Leave the right side edge open.

e. Trim close to the edge of the scallop line, then turn the fabric right-side-out through the open side edge. Press flat.

f. Fold in the raw edges of the open side edge and press flat. Sandwich one end of the grosgrain ribbon into the open seam, then sew the seam shut, catching the ribbon in the seam.

Step 2. Prepare dowel.

a. Wrap each dowel with floral tape. Set aside.

Step 3. Make the flower.

a. Turn the left edge (*without* the ribbon) of the scallop panel in ¾", and then ¾" again. Sew a seam along the top and side to create a pocket for the dowel to slide into.

b. With your embroidery needle and three strands of embroidery floss, sew a running stitch about ¼" from the bottom edge of the scallop panel. Pull the thread tightly to gather the bottom edge. Keep the excess length of thread intact; you'll use this in step 3e.

c. Slide the dowel into the pocket.

d. Wrap the gathered fabric around the dowel to create the layers of the rose. You might have to wrap the fabric in a tight spiral to prevent bulkiness at the bottom.

e. Re-thread the excess length of floss onto your needle and take a few stitches through the base of the flower from side to side to hold it in place.

f. Wrap the length of ribbon around the base of the flower, which will be open at the bottom. Stitch the end of the ribbon in place with three hand-stitches, then cut the end of the ribbon at an angle to finish.

MATERIALS LIST

fabric

Use 44"-wide coordinating prints of light- to mid-weight cotton

Fabric A: ½ yard for the exterior

Fabric B: ½ yard for the interior

other supplies

One yard 1"-wide grosgrain ribbon

Three 12" wooden dowels

Embroidery floss

Embroidery needle

Fabric pencil

Floral tape

Hand sewing needle

Iron & ironing board

Rotary cutter & cutting mat

Ruler

Sewing machine

Sewing thread in coordinating color

Scissors

Straight pins

Scallop pattern (on pattern insert)

PROJECT NOTES

➤ All seams are ¼" unless otherwise stated.

butterfly
MOBILE

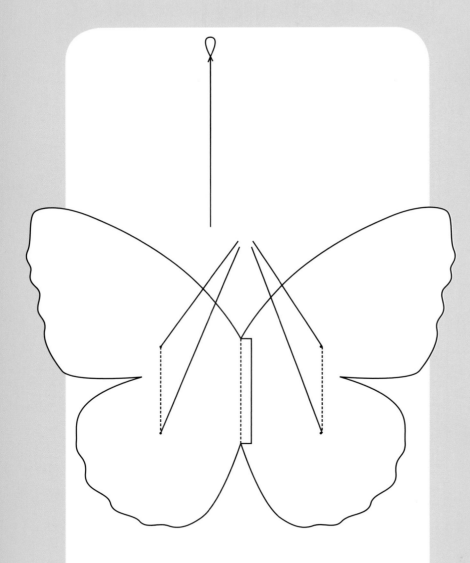

DIAGRAM 1

MATERIALS LIST

fabric

Use 44"-wide coordinating prints of light- to mid-weight cotton

2 yards total of various fabric

2 yards fusible interfacing

other supplies

1" craft brush

12" length of plastic drywall corner bead (available at home improvement stores)

15" embroidery hoop

80" coordinating ribbon

Acrylic paint (to coordinate with fabric selection)

Bone folder / scoring tool

Carbon transfer paper

Craft knife

Craft glue

Cutting mat

Drapery clips (small)

Fishing line (clear)

Large sewing needle

Mat board

Metal ring

Scissors

Butterfly mobile templates (on pattern insert)

Step 1. Prepare fabric pieces and apply fusible interfacing.

a. Cut four 12" × 18" pieces of fabric out of coordinating prints for large-sized Butterfly Pattern A.

b. Cut four 9" × 13" pieces of fabric out of coordinating prints for medium-sized Butterfly Pattern B.

c. Cut eight 6" × 9" pieces of fabric out of coordinating prints for the two small-sized Butterfly Pattern C.

d. Cut the same size and amount of fusible interfacing and apply to all fabric pieces.

Step 2. Prepare butterfly shapes from mat board.

a. Using carbon transfer paper, trace Butterfly Pattern A onto the mat board.

b. Repeat once for Butterfly Pattern B and twice for Butterfly Pattern C.

c. Using a sharp and sturdy craft blade, cut the four butterfly shapes out of mat board.

d. With the bone folder, score a fold line vertically down the center of each butterfly shape and then fold the butterfly wings until they reach approximately 90°.

e. Cut one 4" (large butterfly), one 3" (medium butterfly), and two 2" (small butterfly) lengths of plastic drywall corner bead. You'll use these to reinforce the folded edges of the butterfly shapes.

f. Apply craft glue to the inner side of the drywall corner bead and then cradle the folded mat butterfly shapes into their respective drywall corner bead pieces. Apply pressure until they are fully adhered. Set aside and let dry.

Step 3. Cut butterfly shapes from fabric.

a. Collect all fabric pieces fused with interfacing. Trace the butterfly shapes on the interfacing side of the fabric pieces. For each butterfly, trace two of each wing pattern in coordinating fabrics—two Wing A1 patterns and two Wing A2 patterns, one for each side of the butterfly. Each butterfly will have four fabric pieces.

b. Cut Wings B1, B2, C1 and C2 as you did on Wings A1 and A2.

Step 4. Paint butterfly edges.

a. Paint the edges of the mat board and approximately ½" on the top and bottom surface all the way around the butterfly's edges.

Step 5. Position and glue fabric pieces to mat board.

a. Starting on the underside of the mat butterfly, apply (brush out) a conservative amount of craft glue on the half where the Wing A1 fabric piece should be positioned. The Wing A1 piece has a ½" tab that will be covered by the Wing A2 piece to provide a clean.

b. Apply glue to the uncovered half and position Wing A2 being careful to align all edges and position the edge of the piece along the butterfly's center line to ensure a clean seam.

c. Turn the butterfly over and repeat steps a and b for the topside of the butterfly.

d. Repeat these same steps for all remaining butterflies. Let dry.

Step 6. Suspend each butterfly.

a. Following the pin hole positions indicated on the butterfly patterns, mark pin hole placement on the underside of each butterfly.

b. Using a large sewing needle, thread two separate pieces of clear fishing line through the marks as shown in diagram 1 (page 34).

c. Hold all four ends of the fishing line and allow the butterfly to hang. Level it out to the desired position and tilt.

d. Once the desired position is achieved, create a knot to secure all ends.

e. Finish by attaching a piece of fishing line at the desired length you would like the butterfly to hang (vary the length for each butterfly). Create a knotted loop at the top the line to secure to a drapery clip. Refer to diagram 1 (page 34).

f. Repeat these same steps for all remaining butterflies.

Step 7. Prepare mobile hoop.

a. Cut four equal strips of ribbon approximately 16"-18" long.

b. Using the solid wooden ring from an embroidery hoop, knot or glue each ribbon piece at equal distances apart around the hoop to suspend the hoop evenly in the air. Apply a bead of glue on the inside of the hoop surface and then apply a ribbon end, holding it in place until the ribbon adheres to the hoop. Once the ribbon is firmly in place, wrap it tightly around the hoop two to three times.

c. Bring the ends of all four ribbons together and secure to the metal ring.

Step 8. Attach butterflies.

a. Secure each butterfly to a drapery clip.

b. Clip each butterfly on to the hoop. Space the butterflies so that the hoop hangs level.

c. Finally, hang your butterfly mobile in a place of your choosing.

modern tee
APPLIQUÉ

MATERIALS LIST

fabric

Two 6" × 9" coordinating fabric squares

Double-sided fusible backing

other supplies

One 11" × 17" transparency

One 8" × 10" piece of glass

Craft knife

Fabric pencil

Fabric paint, or acrylic paint with
    textile medium

Heated stencil cutter

Iron & ironing board

Masking tape

Scissors

Sewing machine

Sewing thread in coordinating color

Sponge or craft paint roller

Background design (select from templates
    pages 121-123)

Appliqué design (select from templates
    pages 121-123)

PROJECT NOTES

➢ Preshrink the T-shirt by washing and drying it before
starting your project.

Step 1. Prepare stencil.

a. Select a design as the background pattern for your T-shirt. I used the template on page 123.

b. Place your printed design on your work surface. Next, place the piece of glass on top of the printed design, followed by the clear transparency.

c. Tape all four corners of the transparency down to secure it in place.

d. Using a stencil cutter, cut out the design from the transparency. Make sure to leave enough connections to ensure that the cut stencil retains its form.

Step 2. Stencil background design on T-shirt.

a. Determine the placement of the background design on the T-shirt.

b. Prepare the stencil by spraying a light dusting of spray adhesive on its reverse side and adhere it to the T-shirt where desired.

c. Select a color and apply the fabric paint using a sponge or roller through the stencil onto the T-shirt.

d. Let the paint dry sufficiently, then heat-set it with an iron before washing the shirt for the first time.

Step 3. Cut and prepare appliqué shape.

To see technique demonstrated, refer to page 23.

a. Select an appliqué design that complements the background design and coordinating fabrics. I used the template on page 122.

b. Apply fusible backing to the *wrong* side of the fabric.

c. Trace the design or pin the template to the fusible interfacing side of the fabric. If your design is asymmetrical, you may need to reverse the design, or trace it on the *right* side of the fabric so that it faces the correct direction.

d. Cut out the shape.

Step 4. Appliqué design on T-shirt.

a. Peel the backing from the fusible interfacing.

b. Determine the placement for the appliqué design, and then fuse it into place.

c. Using a traditional tight zigzag stitch, or another tight stitch of your choosing, appliqué the design onto the T-shirt.

pajama
PANTS

PROJECT NOTES

➤ Preshrink your fabric by washing, drying and pressing it before starting your project.

➤ All seams are ⅝" unless otherwise stated.

Step 1. Cut pajama pieces.

a. Fold fabric A in half on the crosswise grain (folded piece will measure 44" × 1¼ yards). Lay the pajama front and back pieces side-by-side, in the same direction, along the lengthwise grain and cut out.

b. Use a fabric marker to transfer all pattern marks to the fabric.

Step 2. Make buttonholes.

To see this technique demonstrated, refer to page 19.

a. On the inside top of each pajama front (where indicated on the pattern), apply a 1" square remnant of fusible interfacing over the buttonhole area.

b. Make a buttonhole in each front where indicated by the pattern marks.

Step 3. Sew pajama front and back together.

a. *Right* sides facing, pin one front and one back piece at the inner leg seams, matching the notches and small dots. Stitch the pieces together. Press the seam.

b. Repeat for the other front and back pieces.

c. With *right* sides of above leg pieces facing, pin the center seam from center front waistline, across crotch, to center back waistline , matching the inner leg seams and notches. Stitch. To reinforce the seam, stitch again over the first line of stitching. Trim the seam in the curved area to ¼". Press the remaining seam open.

d. *Right* sides facing, stitch the front to the back at the side seams.

e. Hem the pant legs to the desired length.

Step 4. Sew contrast fabric casing to waistline.

a. Cut two pieces of the contrast fabric (B). Each piece should be one half the waist measurement in length, plus 1¼" (for seam allowance), and 3¾" wide.

b. *Right* sides facing, sew the short sides of the contrast pieces together.

c. Fold the bottom edge of the contrast piece under ⅝" and iron.

d. *Right* sides facing, pin the raw edge of the contrast facing to the raw edge of the pants waistline. Stitch the seam and press. (The contrast facing will become the waist casing for the elastic and drawstring.)

Step 5. Add elastic to waist.

a. Measure a piece of 1" elastic around your waist. Overlap the ends of the elastic 2" and sew together.

b. Pin the elastic to the inside of the waist casing (made in step 3) evenly. Stretching elastic as necessary. Make sure you place pins on the *right* side of the contrast fabric.

Step 6. Attach contrast pieces to pant cuffs.

a. Cut four pieces of contrast fabric (B), each one half of the bottom pant leg measurement in length, plus 1¼" (for seam allowance), and 4¼" wide.

b. Sew the short ends of two pant cuff contrast pieces together. Repeat on two remaining pieces. Press under both long edges of the pant cuffs ⅝".

c. Pin the *wrong* side of the cuff to the *right* side of the pant leg. Topstitch around the bottom and top of the cuff.

Step 7. Sew pant drawstring.

To see this technique illustrated, refer to Diagram A on page 107.

a. Cut a 2" × 36" piece of the contrast fabric (B).

b. Lay the strip wrong-side-up. Fold under the long, raw edges ½", so the raw edges hit the center, and press to crease. *Wrong* sides facing, fold the entire strip in half lengthwise so that the raw edges are tucked inside. Press.

c. Fold the raw ends in ¼" and topstitch in place.

d. Topstitch along the long, open edge of the drawstring, close to the folded edges.

e. Attach a safety pin to one end of the drawstring and feed it through one of the buttonholes. Continue feeding the drawstring through the casing until you can pull it out through the other buttonhole.

farmer's market
TOTE

PROJECT NOTES

➢ All seams are ½" unless otherwise stated. (The ½" seam
   allowance is included in all of the cutting measurements and
   the pattern pieces.)

Step 1. Cut out pattern pieces.

Lay pattern pieces on the fabric following the lengthwise grain.

a. Cut out two of the main panel pieces from exterior fabric A and two lining pieces from fabric B and two lightweight interfacing pieces.

b. Cut two side panels (each) out of fabrics B and C and the lightweight interfacing.

c. Cut one bottom panels (each) out of fabrics B and C and the heavy-weight interfacing.

Step 2. Sew the lining.

a. Press the end of the left-hand strap under ½" on both of the lining's main panel pieces.

b. With *right* sides facing, stitch one side panel of the lining to each side of one main panel of the lining. Repeat for remaining lining main and side panels.

c. Press the seams open.

Step 3. Attach interfacing to exterior panels.

a. Iron the main panel's fusible interfacing pieces onto the *wrong* side of the exterior main panels.

b. Repeat step 3a for the side panels.

c. Trim ½" off the edges of the bottom interfacing piece. Center and pin the interfacing in the middle of the *wrong* side of the bottom panel. Stitch together ¼" from the interfacing edge.

Step 4. Sew the exterior.

a. Press the end of the right-hand strap under ½" on both of the exterior's main panel pieces.

b. With *right* sides facing, sew the main panel and side panel pieces together as you did in step 2.

Step 5. Sew lining to exterior.

a. *Right* sides facing, pin the lining and exterior fabrics together, matching all seams and curves, keeping raw edges even. Stitch the two layers together along the top edge of the bag and straps. Leave the strap ends and bottom open. Trim the seams; clip curves.

b. Turn the bag right-side-out; press. Insert the raw end of the strap into the pressed end of the strap. Stitch across the strap close to the pressed edge. Topstitch ¼" around the top edge of the bag and all strap edges.

Step 6. Sew bottom.

a. Turn the bag inside out and pull the lining away from the exterior. Attach the lining main panel and the lining bottom panel. *Right* sides facing, pin the main panel to the bottom panel. Stitch around all four sides, ⅜" from the raw edges.

b. Leave the bag inside out. *Right* sides facing, sew three sides of the bottom exterior panel to the exterior main panel, leaving one short side open.

c. Pull the bag through the bottom opening to turn the bag right-side-out.

d. Hand-stitch the bottom opening closed using a blindstitch.

yoga mat
CARRIER

PROJECT NOTES

➤ All seams are ½" unless otherwise stated. (The ½" seam allowance is included in all of the cutting measurements.)

➤ Preshrink your fabric by washing, drying and pressing it before starting your project.

Step 1. Cut all pieces from fabric.

"Long" measurements follow lengthwise grain.

a. Cut a 23¼" (long) × 16½" piece out of fabric A.

b. Cut pocket and flap patterns from fabric B.

c. Cut a 32" (long) × 8" piece of fabric B.

d. Cut a 7" (long) × 16½" piece of fabric C.

e. Cut a 6" circle from fabric C.

f. Cut a 2" (long) × 20" piece of fabric C.

Step 2. Sew Carrier Panels together.

a. *Right* sides facing, sew carrier bag (fabric A) to bottom border (fabric C, see 2d) along the 16½" edges. Press the seam open.

b. To form the casing for the drawstring, fold over the top raw edge of the carrier ¼" and press. Fold over again 1"; press.

c. To reinforce casing for buttonhole, open casing and fuse 1" × ¾" piece of interfacing cantered over the fold line, at the midpoint of the carrier.

d. Fold the casing over to the *wrong* side and stitch close to the bottom folded edge.

Step 3. Sew Pocket.

a. Transfer the fold lines from the pocket pattern onto the fabric.

b. Fold all the raw edges under ¼" (except cut-out corners) and press to the *wrong* side. On the pocket extensions (at the sides and bottom of pocket), fold fabric along marked fold lines in accordion fashion. Press flat. (This creates inverted "pleats" on three sides to allow pocket expansion.)

c. Fold pocket top under ½" (from folded edge) and press to the *wrong* side. Machine-hem close to the fold lines.

d. At each corner of the pocket, with *right* sides facing, stitch a seam connecting the bottom raw edge of the side pocket extension to the side raw edge of the corresponding bottom extension, forming diagonal pocket corners.

e. Position the ¼" fold line of the pocket on the carrier, centered and about 14" from the top. With *right* sides facing, stitch the pocket bottom to the carrier directly over the ¼" fold line.

f. Fold the pocket up on the bottom fold/stitching line and topstitch the pocket sides to the carrier, keeping stitches close to the folded edges, and pleats free of stitching.

g. *Right* sides facing, sew the pocket flap pieces together, leaving an opening on the bottom edge for turning. Turn them right-side-out and press flat. Trim and clip curved seams. Topstitch along the curve edge of the flap.

h. Fold the bottom edge of the flap under ¼" and topstitch it onto the bag above the pocket.

i. *Right* sides facing, sew the sides of the carrier and border together with a ½" seam. Turn the bag right-side-out. Press.

Step 4. Sew Strap.

This technique is illustrated in Diagram A on page 107.

a. Lay the strap piece wrong-side-up. Fold both long, raw edges in 1¾", so the raw edges meet in the center, and press. Fold the entire strip in half lengthwise, *wrong* sides facing, and press. The strap will be about 3" wide.

b. Topstitch along each edge.

c. Fold the ends of the strap under 2". Pin in place, centered along the seam, the top about ½" from the casing stitch line, the bottom about 2½" from the bottom raw edge. Topstitch in place. (See Diagrams A and B on page 87 for more detail.) You might have to remove the extension table on your sewing machine to fit the bag onto the machine.

d. Turn the bag inside out again.

Step 5. Sew bottom of bag and tie.

a. Sew the circle piece onto the bottom of the bag.

b. Follow steps 7a through 7e on page 44 to sew the 2" × 20" piece of fabric into a drawstring.

c. Cover a button with a fabric of your choice (see the technique demonstrated on page 20). Sew the button onto the front of the pocket flap.

d. Hand sew the top of a snap on the underside of the pocket flap. Sew the bottom of the snap to the front of the pocket where it will meet the top snap.

teddy
BEAR

MATERIALS LIST

fabric

Use 44"-wide, mid- to heavy-weight coordinating cotton prints

Fabric A: ¾ yard for the bear

Fabric B: ⅛ yard for ear and paw accents

other supplies

Chalk pencil or fabric marker

Chopstick or wooden dowel

Embroidery floss in dark brown

Embroidery needle

Fiberfill

Hand sewing needle

Iron & ironing board

Scissors

Sewing machine

Sewing thread in coordinating color

Straight pins

Teddy Bear pattern (on pattern insert)

PROJECT NOTES

➤ All seams are ¼" unless otherwise stated. (The ¼" seam allowance is included in all of the cutting measurements and the pattern piece.)

➤ If you want to be able to wash the bear in the future, preshrink your fabric by washing, drying and pressing it before starting your project.

Step 1. Cut all pieces from the fabric.

a. Fold fabric A in half lengthwise, *right* sides together. Lay the pattern pieces on the fabric, and trace. Transfer all marks and lines of construction, then cut out the pieces for the front, back and pocket. (Folding the fabric in half lengthwise will give you a right and left piece for the front and back. You only need one pocket piece.)

b. Cut the ear and paw accent pattern pieces out of fabric B.

Step 2. Sew bear front and pocket.

a. Stitch the dart in each front section of the head. Slash dart to within ¼" of the inner point. Press the dart open. (See this technique demonstrated on page 21.)

b. *Right* sides facing, stitch the front sections of the bear together at the center front.

c. Fold the bottom of the ear accent pieces under ¼" and press. Position the ear accent pieces right-side-up over the ears on the *right* side of the bear front. Topstitch in place close to the fold.

d. As you did with the ears, fold the hand paw accent pieces under ¼" and iron. Topstitch them onto the bear front paw areas.

e. Fold the top edge of the pocket under ¼" and press, then fold under another ¼" and iron to hide the raw edge. Topstitch close to the fold.

f. Fold the bottom edge of the pocket under ¼" and press. With the *wrong* side of the pocket facing the *right* side of the bear front, pin the pocket to the bear front, matching the side edges, and sew along the sides and bottom of the pocket.

Step 3. Embroider bear face

a. Use a chalk pencil to lightly mark the placement of the eyes, nose and mouth.

b. Thread an embroidery needle with three strands of floss. Use a satin stitch (see page 13) to embroider the eyes and nose of the bear.

c. Use a backstitch (see page 12) to embroider the mouth.

Step 4. Sew bear back.

a. Stitch a dart on each back piece (see page 21). Press the dart open.

b. Stitch the back sections together at the center back, leaving an opening between the center back two circles.

Step 5. Sew front and back pieces together and finish.

a. With *right* sides together, pin the front of the bear to the back, matching the symbols and keeping the edges even. Stitch around the edge, leaving the bottom of the feet open. Clip around the curves.

b. Sew the feet paw accent pieces onto each leg following step 2c instructions.

c. Turn the bear right-side-out.

d. Stuff the bear with fiberfill, starting with the arms and legs, then stuffing the head and body. Use the chopstick or dowel to push fiberfill into extremities.

e. Hand sew the back opening closed.

at home

When it comes to decorating any space, the use of fabric is fundamental to the atmosphere you are trying to create. Your personality and style will be reflected in the colors, patterns and textures you use. Combine these design elements with handmade decorative accessories, and you will truly have achieved a unique, inviting area in your home.

The projects in this section provide a variety of ideas for infusing that personal touch into any space. Your statement may be as bold as upholstering a vintage chair, or more subtle by adding a small decorative accessory, such as a framed piece of fabric art. Whether your style is modern, traditional, vintage or a mix of all three, your sensibilities will be inspired in the pages ahead.

fabric collage
LETTER

Step 1. Cut fabric pieces.

a. Cut a variety of square and rectangle fabric pieces.

b. For the pieces to fit around the curves of the letter, cut the sides so that they angle in at the bottom. You can also make a small cut from the center of the bottom to where it meets the letter and fold the fabrics on top of each other.

c. Begin laying out the fabric in a pattern you like, placing the larger pieces first.

d. Fill in the open spaces with smaller pieces of fabric.

Step 2: Glue fabric.

a. Once you are happy with the arrangement of fabric, begin gluing the pieces around the curves first. Apply glue to the *wrong* side of the fabric with a paintbrush. Make sure all the edges are completely glued down so they won't fray.

b. Cut any fraying strings as you go.

MATERIALS LIST

fabric
A variety of coordinating fabric scraps

other supplies
Large, papier mâché letter

Decoupage medium

Paintbrush

Cutting mat

Rotary cutter

PROJECT NOTES

➤ It is easiest to start working the fabric pieces around the curves of the letter first and then place the larger pieces on the letter next.

reversible
TABLE WRAP & NAPKINS

Step 1. Cut table wrap out of fabric and sew hem.

a. Cut two 63" × 21" pieces from both fabrics A and B.

b. On both fabrics A and B, measure 3" in from each corner. Mark, and cut on the diagonal through the mark.

c. Iron each edge of the wrap under ½", and then another ½".

d. Place pieces A and B, *wrong* sides facing , lining up the folded, pressed edges, and pin them in place.

e. Topstitch A to B ¼" from folded edges.

Step 2. Cut napkins from fabric and sew hem.

a. Cut two 21" squares from fabric C.

b. Fold the edges under ½", then another ½" and press. Topstitch in place close to the fold.

Step 3. Embroider napkins.

a. Thread your embroidery machine with contrasting embroidery thread.

b. Follow the machine's instructions for setting up an embroidery frame.

c. Iron a piece of fusible interfacing to the *wrong* side of the napkin behind where the embroidery will be sewn.

d. Follow the machine's instructions for transferring the embroidery design to the fabric.

e. Trim the interfacing close to the stitching.

PROJECT NOTES

➤ If you don't have an embroidery machine, hand embroider the napkins for an equally attractive look.

➤ All seams are ½" unless otherwise stated. (The ½" seam allowance is included in all of the cutting measurements.)

MATERIALS LIST

fabric

Use 44"-wide, mid- to heavy-weight coordinating cotton prints

Fabric A: 2 yards

Fabric B: 2 yards

Fabric C: ¼ yard

other supplies

Coordinating thread

Contrasting thread for embroidery

Lightweight fusible interfacing

Scissors

Straight pins

Cutting mat

Rotary cutter

Sewing machine

Iron and ironing board

Fabric pencil or marker

Embroidery sewing machine

Embroidery designs from Joel Dewberry Designer Embroidery and Thread Collection, by FreeSpirit Fabrics

framed
FABRIC ART

Step 1. Decorative mat covering.

a. Measure and cut a 22" fabric square of fabric to cover the mat board.

b. Place the fabric on a solid surface, right-side-down.

c. Apply a light dusting of spray adhesive to the front of the mat board. Position the mat board on the fabric. Apply even pressure to ensure adhesion. Flip over and gently rub the fabric down onto the mat board surface.

d. Turn the mat board face down so the photo opening is visible.

e. With a ruler, measure ¾" from the edge of the opening and mark a line on the fabric on all four sides.

f. With a craft blade and ruler, cut along the line (on the fabric) to create an open window. Next, make diagonal cuts into the fabric at each corner to within ¹⁄₁₆" of the mat board corner.

g. Apply a path of quick-setting craft glue onto the mat board around the photo opening ½" from the edge.

h. Gently pull the fabric edge back and around the mat board edge, securing it to the glue with even pressure.

i. To complete the mat preparation, trim the outer fabric edges with a craft blade, using the outside edge of the mat board as your guide.

Step 2. Reassemble.

a. Add artwork or a photo of your choosing to the mat board. (For glass etching, refer to pages 24 and 66.)

b. Replace the glass in its proper position followed by the shadow frame spacer and then the mat board / embroidery art construction. Finally, secure the back of the frame in its locked position.

MATERIALS LIST

fabric
¾ yard (44"-wide) light- to mid-weight cotton print

other supplies
20" × 20" shadowbox frame with photo mat board

Craft blade

Ruler

Graphite paper

Fabric pencil

Contact paper

Etching cream

Spray adhesive

Quick-setting craft glue

glass-etched
FABRIC ART

Step 1. Framed fabric art.

a. Measure and cut a 12½" fabric square to be used as the framed art.

b. Position and tape the fabric square to the reverse side of the mat board centered in the photo opening.

Step 2. Glass etching.

To see this technique demonstrated, turn to page 24.

a. Take the glass out of the frame.

b. Apply contact paper to the front surface of the glass. Make sure there are no air bubbles.

c. Select a simple silhouette design of your choice (see pages 120-125). Using graphite paper, trace the design into the desired position on the contact paper.

d. Using a craft blade, cut along the outside edge of the design. Peel off the positive image of the design, exposing the glass in those areas.

e. Apply an etching cream (following the manufacturer's instructions for time and cleaning).

f. Dry the glass surface and set it aside.

Step 3. Reassemble.

a. Replace the glass in its proper position followed by the shadow frame spacer and then the mat board / embroidery art construction. Finally, secure the back of the frame in its locked position.

MATERIALS LIST

fabric
½ yard (54"-wide) light- to mid-weight cotton print

other supplies
20" × 20" shadowbox frame with photo mat board

Craft blade

Ruler

Graphite paper

Pencil

Contact paper

Etching cream

Craft brush

Spray adhesive

Quick-setting craft glue

bird
SACHET

MATERIALS LIST

fabric

Use 44"-wide, light- to mid-weight coordinating cotton prints

Fabric A: one 20" square

Fabric B: one 5" × 10" piece

Fabric C: one 6" × 8" piece

other supplies

Coordinating thread

8"-long piece of cording, ribbon or other fiber to coordinate with fabric

Embroidery floss

Scissors

Polyester fiberfill

Straight pins

Chalk pencil or fabric marker

Two 5mm wooden beads

Embroidery needle

Hand sewing needle

Potpourri (optional)

Sewing machine

Bird pattern (on pattern insert)

PROJECT NOTES

➤ This project works well as a scented sachet, but it can also be used as a pin cushion or an ornament.

➤ All seams are ¼" unless otherwise stated. (The ¼" seam allowance is included in all of the cutting measurements and the pattern piece.)

➤ Preshrink your fabric by washing, drying, and pressing it before starting your project.

Step 1. Cut all pieces from fabric and transfer markings.

To make one bird:

a. Cut two bird body pieces out of fabric A.

b. Cut one bird belly piece out of fabric B.

c. Cut two wing 1 and two wing 2 pieces out of fabric C.

d. Transfer all pattern markings to the fabric pieces with a chalk pencil.

Step 2. Embroider and sew wings.

a. Set aside one wing 1 and one wing 2 piece. These are the wing tops you'll embroider in steps 2b through 2e.

b. Thread your needle with three strands of embroidery floss and bring it up from the bottom of the fabric on the left edge of the curved line you transferred.

c. Sew a stem stitch (see page 17) along that curved line.

d. Knot your thread on the back side of the wing.

e. Repeat steps b–d for the other wing top.

f. Sew one embroidered wing top to its matching bottom with *right* sides facing and using a ¼" seam allowance. Leave a ¾" opening along the straight edge of the wing to turn it.

g. Use a pencil or a seam ripper to help you turn the wing and push the corners out flat. Press the open edge of the wing under ¼" so that the edge is flush with the sewn part of the wing.

h. Using three strands of embroidery floss, sew a blanket stitch (see page 16) along the entire outside edge of the wing.

i. Repeat steps f–h for the second wing.

Step 3. Sew wings and eyes to bird body.

a. Place one wing on the body of the bird where indicated in the pattern.

b. Using regular thread, hand-stitch the tip of the wing that is closest to the head to the body, using a straight stitch that goes around the edge of the wing between the wing and the embroidered blanket stitch. Use about 10 stitches to secure the wing in place.

c. Repeat steps a and b for the other wing.

d. Hand sew a wooden bead onto each side of the bird body where indicated on the pattern.

Step 4. Sew bird together.

a. *Right* sides facing, pin one side of the bird body to the belly piece, matching the pattern markings.

b. Use a ¼" seam allowance to sew the pieces together.

c. *Right* sides facing, pin the other bird body piece to the belly piece at the pattern markings.

d. *Right* sides facing, pin the center head/center back seam of the two body pieces. If you are including a hanging ribbon or cording, make a loop and pin it between the two body layers, about midpoint at the back. The loose ends of the ribbon should be at the raw edge; the loop of the ribbon should lay on the inside of the bird, between the right-side layers.

e. Begin sewing from the base of the bird on the left side, continuing up around the beak, over the top of the head, and back down across the back of the bird to the tail. As you sew over the ribbon, you may want to reinforce the stitch by backstitching. Leave about a 2" opening along the base so you can turn the bird right-side-out and stuff it.

Step 5. Finish bird.

a. Turn the bird right-side-out. You will need to use a sharp object, like a seam ripper or even a pencil, to help you push the beak and tail out flat.

b. If you will be using the bird as a sachet, place the desired amount of potpourri inside the bird. Stuff the bird with fiberfill as tightly as possible, using the seam ripper or a pencil to push fiberfill into the beak and tail.

c. To close, thread the needle, turn the raw edge of the opening under ¼" and hand sew the opening.

flower appliqué
PILLOW

fabric

Use 44"-wide, light- to mid-weight coordinating cotton prints

Fabric A: ¼ yard

Fabric B: ⅛ yard

Fabric C: ⅛ yard

Fabric D: ¼ yard

Fabric E: ⅓ yard

Fabric F: ¼ yard

2¼ yards (10mm) cording

other supplies

Coordinating thread

Lightweight fusible interfacing

Scissors

Straight pins

20" × 20" pillow form

Cutting mat

Rotary cutter

Hand sewing needle

Fabric pencil or marker

Sewing machine

Zipper or cording foot

Flower appliqué template on page 125

PROJECT NOTES

➤ All seams are ¼" unless otherwise stated. (The ¼" seam allowance is included in all of the cutting measurements.)

➤ If you are using fabric that is directional, you will need to increase the amount of fabric by ¼ yard.

➤ If you don't have an embroidery machine, hand embroider the pillow using a blanket stitch (see page 16).

Step 1. Cut all pieces for pillow front and back.

a. Cut one 20" × 7½" piece out of fabric A for the pillow front's center.

b. Cut two 20" × 3" pieces out of fabric B to go on either side of the pillow front center piece.

c. Cut two 20" × 4½" pieces out of fabric C for the edges of the pillow front.

d. Cut one 20" square of fabric E for the back of the pillow.

Step 2. Sew pillow front pieces.

a. Sew both pieces of fabric B to either side of fabric A. Press seams open.

b. Sew both pieces of fabric C to each raw edge of fabric B. Press the seams open.

Step 3. Cut out and sew appliqué pieces.

a. Trace the flower pattern three times onto fabric D with a fabric marker.

b. Iron a piece of fusible interfacing behind each flower.

c. Cut out the flower pieces.

d. Pin the flower pieces to the pillow front where desired.

e. Sew each flower piece in place using an appliqué stitch on your sewing machine.

Step 4. Cut out and sew piping.

See this technique demonstrated on page 22.

a. Cut two 1" × 44" strips of fabric F. Sew the pieces together along one short edge. Press the seams open.

b. Place the cording in the center of the *wrong* side of strip of fabric. Trim the fabric strip so it is 1" longer than the cording on each end.

c. Fold strip over cording, *wrong* sides facing, and stitch the seam along the edge of the piping using a zipper foot.

Step 5. Sew front, back and cording of pillow together.

a. *Right* sides facing, pin the pillow front to pillow back, sandwiching the piping between them, lining up all the raw edges. The unattached ends of the piping should fall at the bottom, where you are leaving a 10" opening for turning and stuffing later.

b. Beginning at one side of the opening and using a zipper foot, stitch a ½" seam through all three layers, using the edge of the cording as your guide. Stop stitching about four inches from the end of the cording. Fold the raw edge at one end of the fabric strip under about ¼".

c. Trim the cording just enough to where the fabric overlaps it by ¼"–½". Slide the folded edge of the fabric strip over the raw edge of the other end. Sew in place.

Step 6. Finish pillow.

a. Turn the pillow right-side-out through the opening at the bottom. Insert the pillow form.

b. Hand-stitch the pillow opening closed, catching the remaining cording between the layers.

sparrow
ACCENT PILLOW

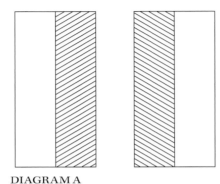

DIAGRAM A

DIAGRAM B

MATERIALS LIST

fabric

Use 44"-wide, light- to mid-weight coordinating cotton prints

Fabric A: ¾ yard

Fabric B: ¾ yard

Fabric C: ¾ yard

Fabric D: ¼ yard

Fabric E: ¼ yard

Fabric F: ¼ yard

Fabric G: ¼ yard

Fabric H: ¼ yard

Fabric I: ¼ yard

Fabric J: ¼ yard

Fabric K: ½ yard

Fusible backing

other supplies

Coordinating thread

One bead for the sparrow's eye

20" × 20" pillow form

Fabric pencil or marker

Scissors

Straight pins

Cutting mat and ruler

Rotary cutter

Sewing machine

Sparrow and leaf patterns on page 126

Scallop pattern (on pattern insert)

PROJECT NOTES

➢ All seams are ¼" unless otherwise stated.

Step 1. Prepare the main fabric pieces.

a. Cut a 20½" × 20½" piece from fabric A for the pillow front.

b. Cut a 20½" × 20½" piece from fabric B for the pillow back.

c. From fabric C, cut four 23" × 4" pieces and two 4" × 16".

d. From fabric K, cut two 4" × 16" strips. The fabric I chose has a linear pattern; I cut on the bias so that each piece could go in a reverse direction.

Step 2. Sew scallop trim details.

a. *Right* sides together, press the four 23" × 4" pieces of fabric C in half lengthwise to make finished pieces that are 23" × 2".

b. With the fold at the top, use a fabric marker (or trace) Scallop Length 1 followed by Scallop Length 2 (with bottoms aligned to the bottom raw edges of the folded fabric) on to each length of Fabric C to create a 20" scallop pattern.

c. Stitch along the traced scallop pattern, leaving ends open.

d. Trim along the outside edge of the stitched line leaving ⅛" margin.

e. Use your scissors to make a snip every ¼" along the margin following the scallop pattern.

f. Turn right-side out and iron flat.

Step 3. Sew leaf pieces.

a. Sew together the two 4" × 16" pieces of Fabric C to the two 4" × 16" pieces of Fabric K. I alternated the orientation of the bias stripe with the solid in each group. Refer to Diagram A on page 76.

b. Back the sewn pieces with double-sided fusible interfacing. Label one sewn piece Leaf combo 1 and the other Leaf combo 2.

Step 4. Cut out sparrow details.

Apply double-sided fusible interfacing to all the fabric pieces that make up the sparrow details.

a. Shape Bird 1: Cut from Fabric F

b. Shape Bird 2: Cut from Fabric D

c. Shape Bird 3: Cut from Fabric K

d. Shape Bird 4: Cut from Fabric I

e. Shape Bird 5: Cut from Fabric G

f. Shape Bird 6: Cut from Fabric H

g. Shape Bird 7: Cut from Fabric J

h. Shape Bird 8: Cut from Fabric E

Step 5. Cut out sparrow details.

For all leaf cuts, align the center seam with the top and bottom points of the leaf pattern. Apply double-sided fusible interfacing to all the leaf fabric pieces.

a. Shape Leaf 1: Cut from Leaf Combo 2

b Shape Leaf 2: Cut from Leaf Combo 2

c. Shape Leaf 3: Cut from Leaf Combo 1

d. Shape Leaf 4: Cut from Leaf Combo 1

e. Shape Leaf 5: Cut from Leaf Combo 2

f. Shape Leaf 6: Cut from Leaf Combo 1

Step 6. Appliqué design to pillow face.

a. Refer to Diagram B on page 76 for placement. Peel off paper backing and fuse each shape in its appropriate position on the pillow front using a hot iron.

b. Using a contrasting color thread, machine appliqué all the leaf and sparrow pieces onto the pillow front.

c. Use the satin stitch setting on the machine to embroider the sparrow legs and feet as well as the branch which should connect all of the leaves.

d. Sew on the bead embellishment for the sparrow's eye.

Step 7. Sew pillow panels and complete.

a. Pin the scallop trim details to the *right* side of the pillow front matching all raw edges.

b. Pin the pillow front and scallop trim combo to the pillow back, *right* sides facing.

c. Stitch the pillow front to the pillow back through all the layers. (The scallops are sandwiched between the front and back.) Leave a sufficient opening at the bottom of the pillow to insert the pillow form.

d. Turn the pillow right-side out, press and insert the pillow form through the opening at the bottom.

e. Hand sew the opening closed.

quilted
THROW

MATERIALS LIST

fabric

Use 50"- or 55"-wide, light- to mid-weight
  coordinating cotton prints

Fabric A: 2½ yards

Fabric B: ⅛ yard

Fabric C: ¼ yard

Fabric D: 1/16 yard

Fabric E: ½ yard

Fabric F: 1/16 yard

Fabric G: Remnant light to mid-weight
  cotton coordinating print (shown as
  orange sunburst print)

Fabric H: ¼ yard

Fabric I: 1½ yards (solid color)

other supplies

Coordinating thread

Scissors

Straight pins

Chalk pencil or fabric marker

Hand sewing needle

Cutting mat and ruler

Rotary cutter

Lightweight batting

Sewing machine

PROJECT NOTES

➤ All seams are ½" unless otherwise stated.

➤ Finished quilt is 50" × 60"

Step 1. Cut all pieces from the fabric.

a. From fabric A, cut one 50" × 60" piece (for quilt back), one 50" × 6" piece, and one 17" × 2½" piece.

b. From fabric B, cut one 13" × 2½" piece and one 50" × 5" piece.

c. From fabric C, cut one 50" × 2½" piece and one 50" × 8" piece.

d. From fabric D, cut one 50" × 2½" and 11" × 2½" piece.

e. From fabric E, cut two 50" × 7" pieces and one 50" × 4" piece.

f. From fabric F, cut one 16" × 4" piece and one 50" × 2½"

g. From fabric G, cut one 8" × 2½" piece.

h. From fabric H, cut one 50" × 9½" piece.

i. From fabric I, cut one 8½" × 2½" piece, one 30½" × 2½" piece, four 50" × 2½" pieces, one 25½" × 4" piece, one 10½" × 4" piece, one 40½" × 2½" piece, one 7½" × 2½" piece, one 36½" × 2½" piece, one 27½" × 2½" piece and one 7½" × 2½" piece.

Step 2. Sew fabric strips together.

a. Refer to Diagram A on page 83. Sew all 19 pieced rows together. Press seams.

b. Working from the top row and working your way down, sew each row to the next. Press seams.

Step 3. Layer the backing, batting and pieced front.

a. Lay the back piece of the quilt on a flat surface and cut a piece of batting to the same size.

b. Lay the pieced top of the quilt over the batting and pin all layers, matching raw edges. Baste all layers together. Remove pins,

Step 4. Machine quilt the throw.

Quilt in every row, except the rows that are 1½" high. (Rows 2-6, 10, 12, 14-16, 18.)

a. Begin in the middle of Row 9 and stitch a vertical line every 1⅜" to one edge of the throw. Repeat on the other half of that row.

b. Quilt Rows 1, 7, 8, 11, 13, 17 and 19 in the same manner as in step 4a.

Step 5. Make the binding for the throw.

a. Cut enough 2" strips out of the remaining fabric to make a continuous binding piece that will be 230" long. Cut the strips on the *bias* grain,

b. *Right* sides facing, stitch the bias strips together at the short ends in ½" seams until the bias strip is 230" long.

Step 6: Attach the binding to the throw.

a. Trim off any excess batting and backing fabric so all the raw edges are even.

b. Fold the starting end of your binding at a 45° angle and press. Fold under on long edge of binding ¼" and press. Then, *wrong* sides facing, fold the binding in half lengthwise (to 1¼") and press. Starting in the middle of one of your quilt sides, pin the unfolded, raw edge of the binding along the edge of the quilt, matching raw edges of the quilt and binding.

c. Begin stitching about 8–10" from the folded end of the binding. Stitch through all layers, leaving the 8–10" of binding unsewn.

d. When you get ¼" from the first corner, backstitch several stitches. Remove the quilt from your machine.

e. Fold the binding back on itself, perpendicular to the seam you just stitched, to form a diagonal fold.

f. Fold the binding again. This time, align the fold in the binding with the raw edges of the seam you just sewed. Align the raw edges of the unstitched binding with the next raw edge of the quilt and stitch the binding to the next side of the quilt, stopping ¼" from the next corner.

g. Repeat steps 6e and 6f for each corner of your quilt.

h. When you are back to the side where you started, starting side, stitch to within 8–10" of the point you began stitching the binding to the quilt.

i. Pin the 8–10" of binding with the folded end along one quilt edge, matching raw edges of the quilt. Trim the raw-edged end so it overlaps the folded end by about 1". Lay this raw edge over the folded end and stitch the binding to the quilt.

k. Fold the binding over the raw edges of the quilt to the back side and hand-stitch the binding fold to the quilt back, just beyond the stitching line. Tuck each corner into a pretty miter as you go.

	Row 1
A (50"× 6")	

I (8"× 2½")	B (13"× 2½")	I (30"× 2½")	Row 2

C (50"× 2½")	Row 3
I (50"× 2½")	Row 4
D (50"× 2½")	Row 5
I (50"× 2½")	Row 6
E (50"× 7")	Row 7

I (25½"× 4")	F (16"× 4")	I (10½"× 4")	Row 8

C (50"× 8")	Row 9

I (40½"× 2½")	D (11"× 2½")	Row 10

E (50"× 4")	Row 11

I (7½"× 2½")	G (8"× 2½")	I (36½"× 2½")	Row 12

B (50"× 5")	Row 13
I (50"× 2½")	Row 14
F (50"× 2½")	Row 15
I (50"× 2½")	Row 16
E (50"× 7")	Row 17

I (27½"× 2½")	A (17"× 2½")	I (7½"× 2½")	Row 18

H (50"× 9½")	Row 19

DIAGRAM A

patchwork
DUVET COVER

PROJECT NOTES

➤ Preshrink your fabric by washing, drying and pressing it before starting your project.

➤ All seams are ½" unless otherwise stated.

➤ Finished size of duvet will be approximately 88" × 99"—about the size of a queen duvet.

➤ All measurements are based on 44"-wide fabrics. For this project, it is best to work with light- to mid-weight cotton. If you are using a fabric with a large scale pattern, such as the Antler Damask, for the duvet's back and want to match up the patterns on the two pieces, you will have to double the yardage of fabric bought.

MATERIALS LIST

fabric

Use 44"-wide, light- to mid-weight coordinating cotton prints

Fabric A: 1 yard

Fabric B: 1 yard

Fabric C: 1 yard

Fabric D: 2 yards

Fabric E: 2 yards

Fabric F: 1 yard

Fabric G: ¾ yard

Fabric H: ⅓ yard

Fabric I: ½ yard

Fabric J: 1 yard

Fabric K: 5 yards

Fabric L: ⅓ yard

Fabric M: ⅓ yard

Fabric N: ⅓ yard

Fabric O: 5 yards

other supplies

Cutting mat

Iron & ironing board

Rotary cutter

Ruler

Scissors

Sewing machine

Sewing thread in coordinating color

Straight pins

Step 1. Cut all pieces from the fabric as indicated below:

a. Fabric A: 34" × 12"; 12" × 12" (two pieces)

b. Fabric B: 12" × 12"; 23" × 23"; 23" × 12"

c. Fabric C: 23" × 23"; 12" × 34"; 23" × 12"; 12" × 12"

d. Fabric D: 12" × 34"; 23" × 23; 34" × 12"; 3¼" × 89 " (two pieces)

e. Fabric E: 12" × 23"; 23" × 23" (two pieces); 34" × 12"

f. Fabric F: 12" × 12" (two pieces); 12" × 34"

g. Fabric G: 12" × 23"; 23 × 12"

h. Fabric H: 12" × 12"

i. Fabric I: 34" × 12"; 12" × 12"

j. Fabric J: 12" × 23"; 12" × 12"; 34" × 12"

k. Fabric K: 23" × 12"; 12" × 12"; 7" × 100" (two pieces for side borders); 39½" × 7" (four pieces for top and bottom borders); 4" × 14¾" (twelve pieces for ties)

l. Fabric L: 23" × 12"; 12" × 12"

m. Fabric M: 12" × 12"

n. Fabric N: 12" × 12" (two pieces)

o. Fabric O: 39½" × 88" (two pieces for duvet back)

Step 2. Sew the pieced side of the duvet cover.

Follow layout diagram at right.

a. Begin with the left column. Sew the cut pieces together to form larger blocks where all the sides are even, then sew large sections together to form the left column of the duvet cover.

b. Sew the middle column of the duvet cover by starting at the top and continuing to work all the way down.

c. Sew the right-hand column of the duvet using the same method.

d. Sew the three columns together to form the full pieced front side of the duvet cover.

Step 3. Sew the back of the duvet cover.

a. *Right* sides facing, pin the long (88") raw edges of two fabric O pieces. Stitch seam and press open.

b. *Right* sides facing, stitch together two of the 39½" × 7" pieces of K together along the short sides forming the top border piece. *Right* sides together, pin the border to the top of the duvet back (3a), matching raw edges, and stitch a seam. Press seam open.

c. Repeat step 3b to form the bottom border.

d. Sew the 7" × 100" pieces of fabric K onto each side of the back piece to form the side borders as did top and bottom.

Step 4. Sew contrast facing to front and back of duvet cover.

a. With *right* sides together, pin one of the 89" × 3¼" fabric D contrast facings to the top edge of the duvet front and the other to the top of the top border. Stitch seams and press open.

b. Repeat step a for the inside contrast piece on the back of the duvet cover.

Step 5. Sew duvet cover ties.

a. Take one of the 4" × 14¾" fabric K pieces, and fold under each long raw edge 1" and press. Fold in half lengthwise, *wrong* sides together, matching folded edges. Topstitch down entire   to both folded edges.

b. Fold one end of the tie under ½", then again another ½". Sew fabric in place to finish the edge.

c. Repeat steps 5a and 5b for all of the tie pieces.

Step 6. Attach ties to duvet cover.

a. Fold under the unfinished end of each of the ties ¾" and press.

b. Pin the folded edge of one of the ties to the *right* side of the contrast facing on the front duvet cover piece. The first tie should be placed 6½" from the side edge as shown in Diagram A.

c. Pin the remaining five ties every 14½" along the edge of the contrast facing or until you are pleased with the spacing of the ties. Repeat steps 6a through 6c on back.

d. Topstitch each tie to facing forming a 1" square with stitching. Topstitch an "X" inside the square to reinforce the tie, as shown in Diagram A on page 87.

e. Fold under the long raw edges of the contrast facing ¼" and press.

f. Fold the contrast facing to the *wrong* side of the duvet, as shown in Diagram B (page 87) and press.

Step 7. Finish duvet cover.

a. With *right* sides together, stitch the sides and bottom of the duvet cover front and back pieces together.

b. Turn the duvet cover right-side-out and press flat.

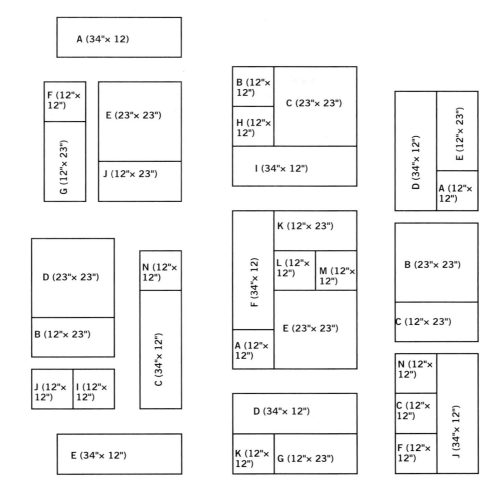

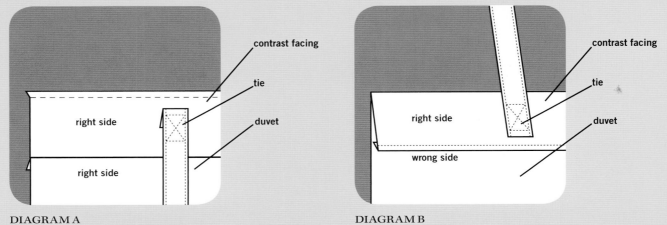

DIAGRAM A

DIAGRAM B

pillowcases

Step 1. Make piping.

To see this technique demonstrated, turn to page 22.

a. Cut four 20½" long pieces of cording.

b. Cut four 21½" × 2" pieces of fabric L to cover the cording.

c. Place a piece of cording in the middle of one of the fabric strips and fold the fabric in half over the cording.

d. Using the zipper foot, stitch fabric using edge of cording as a guide.

e. Repeat steps 1a through 1d for each piece of piping.

Step 2. Sew piping to pillowcase border.

a. Cut four 21½" × 6" pieces of fabric K.

b. Fold under one long edge of the fabric ½" and press.

c. Pin one piping piece to the folded edge of each border piece, placing folded edge of border flush to cording. Using the zipper foot, stitch through all layers to fold.

d. Fold under the top edge of the border ½" and press.

Step 3. Cut and sew pieces for pillowcase.

a. Cut four 21½" × 30½" pieces from the white fabric.

b. Fold under one 21½" edge of each white fabric piece ½" and press.

c. Pin one *wrong* side of border pieces to *right* sides of a white fabric pieces matching the folded edges.

d. Stitch borders to white fabric pieces, keeping stitching close to folded edges. You now have two pillowcase fronts and two pillowcase backs.

Step 4. Finish pillowcase.

a. *Right* sides facing, pine pillowcase fronts to backs, matching raw edges, and stitch seams.

b. Turn the pillowcases right-side-out and press.

MATERIALS LIST

fabric

Use 44"-wide, light- to mid-weight coordinating cotton prints

Fabric K (from duvet cover): ½ yard

Fabric L (from duvet cover): ⅓ yard

2½ yards white solid fabric

2½ yards of ⅛-inch cording

other supplies

Cutting mat

Iron & ironing board

Rotary cutter

Ruler

Sewing thread in coordinating color

Sewing machine

Scissors

Straight pins

Zipper foot

PROJECT NOTES

➤ Preshrink your fabric by washing, drying and pressing it before starting your project.

➤ All seams are ½" unless otherwise stated.

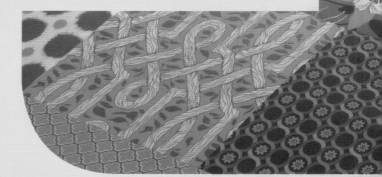

vintage
UPHOLSTERED CHAIR

PROJECT NOTES

➤ The success of this project begins with having a beautiful piece of furniture worth salvaging. A forgotten chair in an attic or garage, or one discovered at a local thrift store or antique dealer, is a prime candidate for your attention.

➤ Focus on finding a chair that has character in the forms of the legs or other unique features in its body that can be accentuated by means of a new paint job, staining or fabric application.

➤ You'll have to adapt these instructions based on the chair you've found.

Step 1. Photograph your subject.

a. To preserve the elements you found most beautiful when you discovered your selected piece, be sure to take a series of photographs from many angles prior to starting your renovation. These photographs serve as a reference point as well as a reminder of the tremendous progress you are making.

Step 2. Disassemble.

a. Strip the chair by removing the upholstery, taking care not to tear any of the pieces as they will be used for patterns in step 5. Use pliers to remove staples and tacks, and use scissors or a seam ripper to separate the upholstery pieces at the seams. Remove the black bottom cloth from the underside of the chair. Next, remove the seat from the chair frame and remove the upholstery fabric from the seat. Using a marker, note the location and orientation of each upholstery piece.

b. Where necessary, replace filling or batting by wrapping batting over the seat top and then pulling and stapling on the reverse side. The chair back cushion can be reinforced in a similar way, but instead of stapling on the reverse side, staple batting to the surface in an area that will be covered by the new upholstery, trim and tacks. To prevent visible indents from the staples, pull gently on the batting around each staple so that the staple is pulled inside the batting. As a general rule, I nearly always add extra new batting to firm up seat, back and arm cushions.

Step 3. Surface prep work.

a. Sand all wood areas, removing previous paint, varnish or lacquer. Sand until a smooth surface is achieved.

b. Wipe the wood down with a damp cloth and leave it to dry.

Step 4. Paint chair body.

a. Apply a primer for durability and to ensure adhesion of the final color. Let it dry sufficiently.

b. Paint the chair body a color that coordinates well with the fabric you've selected. Let dry sufficiently. Repeat until full coverage is achieved.

Step 5. Preparing the upholstery pieces for the chair's back cushion.

a. Lay the original upholstery pieces, right-side-up, on the *right* side of the new upholstery fabric (A for the front pieces and fabric D for the back pieces).

b. Cut the fabric, leaving 2–3" of excess fabric beyond the edges of the original pieces; this will allow for grasping the fabric when stapling.

Step 6. Preparing the upholstery pieces for the chair's seat cushion.

a. Using the original pieces of the seat cushion as a template, trace them onto the new fabric as you did for the back in step 5. Use fabric A for the seat top and fabric C for the seat sides. Cut.

b. Sew enough piping from fabric B, following instructions from page 22, to travel around all sides of the cushion at the top seam (piece 1 of piping) and bottom edge (piece 2 of piping).

c. Pin the first piece of piping (piece 1) to the *right* side fabric for the seat cushion top. Baste.

d. Pin the construction from step 6c, *right* sides facing, to the side panels. Stitch together using a ½" seam.

e. Turn right-side out, ready to fit over the seat cushion.

f. Drape the seat fabric over the seat cushion batting and position it evenly.

g. Holding the cushion and fabric covering securely, turn the cushion upside down and place it on a solid surface.

h. Starting at the front of the cushion, begin pulling the fabric around and stapling it securely. Work your way around the sides and to the back evenly.

i. To complete the seat cushion, position and staple the second piece of piping (piece 2) along the bottom edge of the seat cushion.

Step 7. Reassemble with new upholstery.

a. Place the front fabric (A) piece from step 5 on the chair back. Use upholstery tacks to temporarily tack the fabric in place, then staple at the top of the head rail, down the sides of the upright rails and on the underside of the bottom back rail, pulling the fabric tightly as you staple it in place.

b. Repeat this procedure to apply the back fabric (D) to the backside of the chair back.

c. Finish the stapled edges of the chair back by applying decorative upholstery trim with upholstery tacks over the stapled edges.

d. Reposition and secure the chair seat cushion (from Step 6) to the chair frame.

at work

Your workspaces can also be transformed by the creative use of fabric. Sometimes these hardworking, practical areas are overlooked when it comes to design. Yet, your personal style can still be reflected in creative ways in your office, your kitchen or even your closet.

This section provides a collection of useful, yet stylish sewing projects that will add a bit of personality to any workspace. These fabric-made projects offer unique and useful storage, organization and sensible solutions for a variety of workspaces. Whether you are at work in your kitchen, your office or other workspace, your sense of style and creativity does not have to be compromised for the practical.

journal
COVERS

Step 1. Cut out all fabric pieces for the large journal cover.

   a. Cut one 11¾" × 11¾" piece from fabric A for the main panel of the cover.

   b. Cut two 3¼" × 11¾" pieces from fabric B for the cover front.

   c. Cut two 7¾" × 11¾" pieces from fabric C for the inside cover.

   d. Cut one 15" × 11¾" piece of fabric D for the lining.

   e. Cut one 5¼" × 7¾" piece from fabric A for the inside pocket.

Step 2. Add embroidery.

   a. Thread the embroidery machine with contrasting thread. Follow the machine's instructions for setting up the embroidery frame.

   b. Determine the placement of the embroidery design, then iron a piece of fusible interfacing to the *wrong* side of the main panel (fabric A) behind where the embroidery will be sewn.

   c. Follow the machine's instructions for transferring the embroidery design to the fabric. Trim the interfacing close to the stitching.

PROJECT NOTES

➤ This large journal cover fits an 8½" × 11" journal. This small journal cover fits a 6" × 9½" journal.

➤ If you don't have an embroidery machine, hand embroider the journal cover for an equally attractive look.

➤ All seams are ¼" unless otherwise stated.

MATERIALS LIST

fabric

Use 44"-wide, light- to mid-weight coordinating cotton prints

For large journal cover:

Fabric A: ⅓ yard

Fabric B: ⅓ yard

Fabric C: ⅓ yard

Fabric D: ¼ yard

For small journal cover:

Fabric A: ¼ yard

Fabric B: ⅛ yard

Fabric C: ¼ yard

other supplies

3" of 1"-wide grosgrain ribbon

15" of ¼"-wide grosgrain ribbon

Iron & ironing board

Scissors

Sewing machine

Sewing thread in coordinating color

Small piece of lightweight fusible interfacing

Straight pins

Embroidery machine

Embroidery designs from Joel Dewberry Designer Embroidery and Thread Collection, by FreeSpirit Fabrics

Step 3. Sew the large journal cover.

a. With *right* sides facing, sew a fabric B panel to the one shorter edge of the main panel (fabric A). Sew the other fabric B piece to the other edge of A. Press the seams open.

b. With *right* sides facing, sew one of the fabric C pieces to the shorter edge of fabric B on the front right-hand panel. Press the seams open.

c. Fold under the top of the pocket piece ¼" and then another ¼" and stitch to secure. Press flat.

d. With *right* sides together, sew the pocket piece to the other fabric C piece, lining up the bottom and side edges.

e. Place the pocket panel *right* side down over the front panel, aligning with the front panel's left edge. Pin a small loop of the 1" grosgrain ribbon (just enough to hold a pen in place) between these layers. Sew the pocket panel to the front panel, catching the ribbon in place.

f. Fold each short edge of the interior lining piece (fabric D) under ¼" then another ¼", and stitch to secure.

g. Pin one end of the narrow ribbon to the *right* side of the cover, at the center of the top edge.

h. With *right* sides facing, sew the interior lining piece to the cover, making sure it is centered and catching the ribbon.

i. Turn the cover right-side-out through one of the open sides. Press flat.

j. Fold back each of the inside panels at the seam so that the *right* sides of the flaps are on top of the front panel. Sew at the top and bottom.

k. Turn the fabric so that the *right* side faces out.

Step 4. Cut out all fabric pieces for the small journal cover.

a. Cut two 3½" × 10" piece from fabric A for the sides of the exterior cover on cover front and back.

b. Cut one 4¾" × 6½" piece from fabric A for the inside pocket.

c. Cut one 2½" × 10" piece from fabric B for the cover front inset.

d. Cut one 5½" × 10" piece from fabric C for the cover section that wraps from the front, around the spine.

e. Cut one 11" × 10" piece from fabric C for the inside lining.

Step 5. Add embroidery.

a. Embroider the front panel of the small journal using the instructions for the large journal on page 96.

Step 6. Sew the cover for the small journal.

a. With *right* sides facing, sew the inset (fabric B) panel to the front panel (fabric A). Sew the other edge of fabric B inset to one edge of the fabric C piece that will wrap over the spine to form that main panel of the back cover. Press the seam open.

b. With *right* sides facing, sew the other fabric A piece to the fabric C piece for the back cover. Press the seams open.

c. Fold under the top of the pocket piece ¼" and then another ¼" and stitch to secure. Press flat.

d. With *right* sides together, sew the pocket piece to the back fabric C piece, lining up the bottom and side edges.

e. Place the pocket panel *right* side down over the front panel, aligning with the front panel's left edge. Pin a small loop of the 1" grosgrain ribbon (just enough to hold a pen in place) between these layers. Sew the pocket panel to the front panel, catching the ribbon in place.

f. Fold under each short edge of the interior lining piece (fabric D) ¼" then another ¼", and stitch to secure.

g. Pin one end of the narrow ribbon to the *right* side of the cover, at the center of the top edge.

h. With *right* sides together, sew the interior lining piece to the cover, making sure it is centered and catching the ribbon.

i. Turn the cover right-side-out through one of the open sides. Press flat.

j. Fold back each of the inside panels at the seam so that the *right* sides of the flaps are on top of the front panel. Sew at the top and bottom.

k. Turn the fabric so that the *right* side faces out.

hanger
COZY

MATERIALS LIST

fabric

Use 44"-wide, light- to mid-weight
coordinating cotton prints

Fabric A: ¾ yard

Fabric B: ¼ yard (muslin or cotton print)

other supplies

Three ¾" buttons

Embroidery floss

Embroidery needle

Fabric pencil or marker

Iron & ironing board

Hanger

Scissors

Sewing machine

Sewing thread in coordinating color

Straight pins

Tracing paper

PROJECT NOTES

➤ All seams are ¼" unless otherwise stated. (The ¼" seam
allowance is included in all of the cutting measurements.)

Step 1. Make your pattern.

a. Trace the shape of the hanger onto a piece of tracing paper for a pattern.

b. Add 1" to your pattern on the sides and top. Add 1½" to the bottom edge.

Step 2. Cut out fabric pieces.

a. Cut the front panel of the hanger cozy out of the piece of muslin using the pattern you made as your guide.

b. Fold fabric A in half lengthwise. Place hanger pattern on fabric, and measure down 11" from the bottom (straight) edge of the pattern. This extra 11" will form the hanger cozy's back and the front pocket. Cut out both pieces.

Step 3. Add embroidery.

a. Trace a letter in the middle of the muslin panel with a fabric pencil.

b. Thread an embroidery needle with three strands of floss and use a split stitch (see page 14) to sew the outline on the main body of the letter.

c. Use the three strands of floss to embroider the flowers in the middle of your letter using a lazy daisy stitch (see page 15).

d. Thread your needle with two strands of floss and sew the curlicues on your letter using a backstitch (see page 12).

Step 4. Sew fabric pieces together.

a. Fold under the top edge of each back/pocket panel and the front panel ¼" and then another ¼" and stitch to secure.

b. With *right* sides facing, sew the muslin panel to one of the back/pocket panels along the curved sides.

c. *Right* sides facing, place the other back/pocket panel over the joined front/back piece (4b), matching all raw edges. Stitch together along the curved and (straight) side edges.

d. Turn the panel that's on top over the two other pieces to face right-side-out.

e. Turn the muslin piece over both back panels to face right-side-out. Press flat.

Step 5. Sew pockets.

a. Fold under the bottom edges of the back pocket panel ¾" then another ¾" and press flat. Sew the hem ½" from the edge.

b. Fold the back/pocket panel up to the front to form a pocket, but don't sew it in place yet. Mark 4" from the side edge for the first pocket placement, then another 4" over for the middle pocket.

c. Mark a spot for the placement of each button about ¼" from the hemmed edge of the pocket.

d. Make your buttonholes (see page 19).

e. Sew the buttons on the inside of the pocket. Fold pocket panel back up.

f. Topstitch along the edges of the pocket and along the pocket lines (5b) to finish the pocket.

reversible
FABRIC BOXES

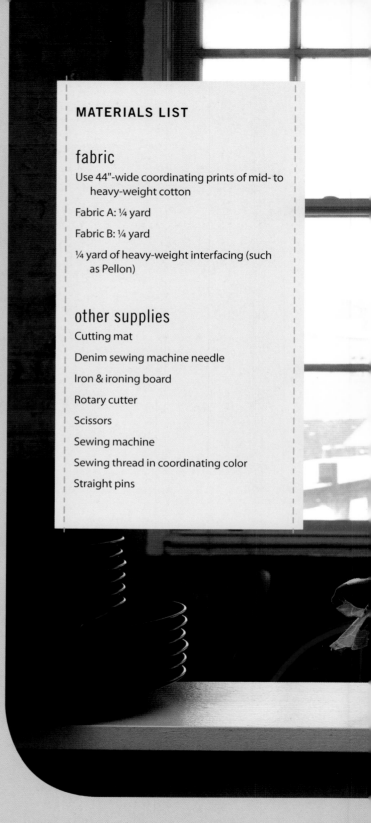

MATERIALS LIST

fabric

Use 44"-wide coordinating prints of mid- to heavy-weight cotton

Fabric A: ¼ yard

Fabric B: ¼ yard

¼ yard of heavy-weight interfacing (such as Pellon)

other supplies

Cutting mat

Denim sewing machine needle

Iron & ironing board

Rotary cutter

Scissors

Sewing machine

Sewing thread in coordinating color

Straight pins

PROJECT NOTES

➤ All seams are ½" unless otherwise stated. (The ½" seam allowance is included in all of the cutting measurements.)

Step 1. Cut fabric pieces from fabric A.

a. Cut one 7" × 7" piece for the bottom.

b. Cut four 7" × 6" pieces for the sides.

c. Cut two 4½" squares, then cut each square diagonally for four triangle pieces.

d. Cut eight 2" × 12" pieces for the ties.

Step 2. Cut fabric pieces from fabric B.

a. Cut one 7" × 7" piece for the bottom.

b. Cut four 7" × 6" pieces for the sides.

c. Cut two 4½" × 4½" squares, then cut each square diagonally for four triangle pieces.

Step 3. Cut pieces from interfacing.

a. Cut one 6" × 6" piece for the bottom.

b. Cut four 5" × 6" pieces for the sides.

Step 4. Sew ties.

a. Follow Diagram A on facing page. Lay one 2" × 12" strip, *wrong* side up. Fold in the long, right-hand edge by ½", so the raw edge hits the center, and press to crease. Repeat with the left side. Fold the entire strip in half lengthwise so that the raw edges are tucked inside. Iron to crease. The strip will be ½" wide.

b. Fold over one raw short edge of the tie and sew in place.

c. Sew along the long, open edge of the tie then topstitch along the folded edge of the tie.

d. Repeat steps 4a–4c for the remaining ties.

Step 5. Sew triangle indents.

a. Refer to Diagram B on the facing page. Take one triangle piece each from fabrics A and B. With *right* sides facing, sew them together along the long edge, using a ¼" seam allowance.

b. Turn the piece right-side-out and press flat.

c. Repeat steps 5a and 5b for the six remaining triangle pieces.

Step 6. Sew outside and inside of box.

a. With *right* sides facing, sew one 7" edge of a fabric A side piece to one edge of the fabric A bottom piece. Press the seam open. Repeat for all four sides of the fabric A bottom piece.

b. Press the three remaining raw edges of each side panel under ½".

c. Repeat steps 6a and 6b for sewing the inside of the box from fabric B.

Step 7. Sew box together.

a. Refer to Diagram B on facing page. Lay the outside piece (fabric A) flat with the *wrong* side up.

b. Center all of the interfacing pieces on the side and bottom pieces, sliding the interfacing beneath the pressed edges of the sides.

c. Lay the inside box piece (fabric B) on top of the interfacing, matching up the edges with the (fabric A) outside box piece. Sandwich a triangle piece in between each of the outside and inside box layers at the corners, as shown, and pin in place.

d. Slide a tie in between the two box layers near the top of each corner and pin in place.

e. Sew the box together by topstitching along each edge of the box, making sure to catch the triangle side pieces and ties as you go.

f. Once the box is sewn together, fold up the sides and tie a bow at each corner to hold them in place.

To make the larger box pictured, follow the above steps but with these measurements:

» Bottom pieces: 9" × 13"

» Side pieces: 9" × 13"

» Triangle pieces: 7" × 7" squares cut on the diagonal

» Cut interfacing 1" smaller than fabric pieces

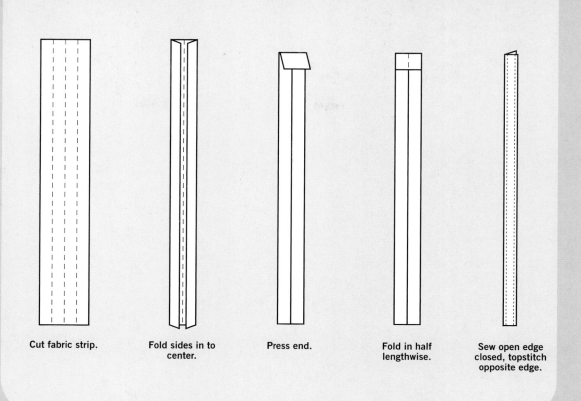

Cut fabric strip.

Fold sides in to center.

Press end.

Fold in half lengthwise.

Sew open edge closed, topstitch opposite edge.

DIAGRAM A

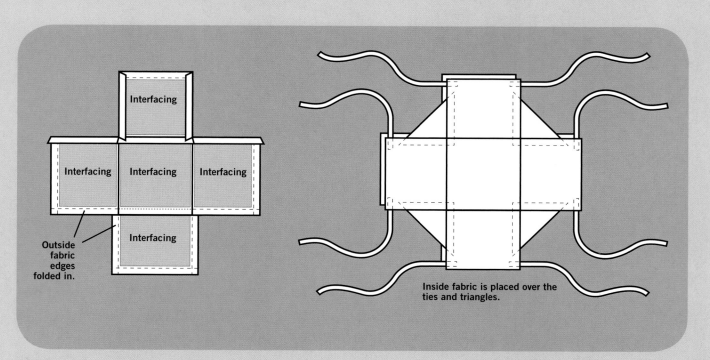

Interfacing

Interfacing   Interfacing   Interfacing

Interfacing

Outside fabric edges folded in.

Inside fabric is placed over the ties and triangles.

DIAGRAM B

office chair
CUSHION

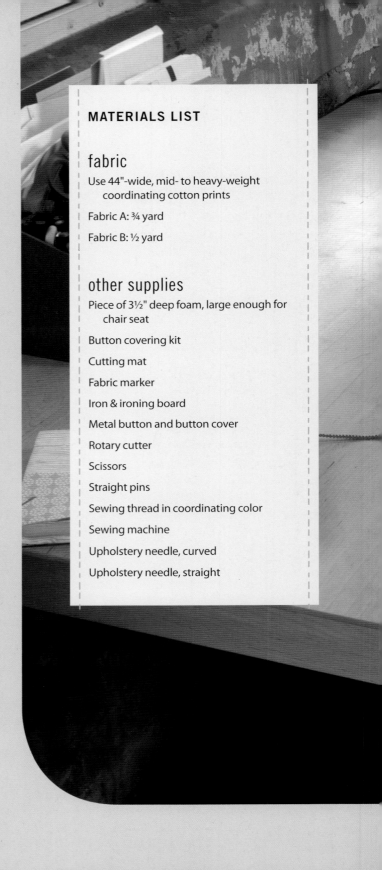

MATERIALS LIST

fabric

Use 44"-wide, mid- to heavy-weight coordinating cotton prints

Fabric A: ¾ yard

Fabric B: ½ yard

other supplies

Piece of 3½" deep foam, large enough for chair seat

Button covering kit

Cutting mat

Fabric marker

Iron & ironing board

Metal button and button cover

Rotary cutter

Scissors

Straight pins

Sewing thread in coordinating color

Sewing machine

Upholstery needle, curved

Upholstery needle, straight

PROJECT NOTES

➤ All seams are ¼" unless otherwise stated. (The ¼" seam allowance is included in all of the cutting measurements.)

Step 1. Create pattern.

a. Trace the chair seat onto paper for a pattern. Add ¼" to the perimeter of the pattern.

Step 2. Trace pattern and cut out cushion pieces.

a. Trace the pattern of the chair seat onto fabric A. Cut two pieces, one for the top and one for the bottom.

b. Cut a piece from fabric B for each side of the cushion; it should be 4" × the length of the sides of the cut cushion pieces.

c. Cut four 2" × 20" pieces of fabric B for the chair ties.

Step 3. Sew ties and cushion pieces together.

a. Fold the long side of the chair ties into the center—left side in by ½", then right-hand side in by ½" and press flat.

b. Fold over one short edge of each tie about ½". Fold the ties in half lengthwise and topstitch around the edges.

c. With *right* sides facing, sew each of the side pieces together at its short edges.

d. With *right* sides together, sew the top cushion piece to the side pieces.

e. Pin two ties on each corner of the back of the cushion cover.

f. With *right* sides facing, sew the bottom of the cushion cover to the sides, catching the ties as you sew. Leave the space in between the ties open for the foam to fit through.

g. Turn cover right-side-out, press and insert foam. Use a blindstitch to hand sew the back of the cushion cover closed.

Step 4. Upholster cushion and add button.

a. Measure in 1" from the perimeter of the cushion on the top, bottom and sides and mark a line with a fabric marker. Make a mark every ½" to use as your guide for stitching.

b. Thread a curved upholstery needle. Starting at the back of the cushion along the upper edge of the side panel, feed your needle through the foam to the top. Bring the needle over to the next mark. Push the needle down to the next mark along the upper edge of the side panel, then back through to the top. Repeat until you have stitched around both the top and the bottom of the cushion, forming a border around cushion too and bottom, as shown.

c. Cover a metal button with fabric B (see page 20). Thread a long upholstery needle and feed the needle through the bottom of the cushion, through the button shank on top and then back down. Tie the strands of thread in a tight knot on the back.

apron

PROJECT NOTES

➤ All seams are ¼" unless otherwise stated. (The ¼" seam
  allowance is included in all of the cutting measurements and
  the pattern piece.)

Step 1. Cut out apron and hem.

a. Using a fabric pencil or marker, trace the apron pattern onto fabric A and cut.

b. Fold under all the edges ¼", then another ¼" and sew in place.

Step 2. Cut and sew neck strap.

a. Cut a 2½" × 21" piece out of fabric B for the neck strap.

b. Fold the neck strap in half lengthwise (*right* sides facing) and sew a ½" seam along the raw edge.

c. Trace a half circle on one end of the strap to create a rounded edge and sew along the traced line. Trim the fabric close to the curved edge. Press the seam open along the long edge.

d. Turn the strap right-side-out through the open end of the strap and press flat, keeping the seam along one side.

e. Align the raw edge of the neck strap along the right side of the apron front, at the top left edge. Sew together. Fold the top of the apron to the back another ½" and sew in place, hiding the raw edge of the tie under the fold.

f. Turn the apron over and topstitch along the upper edge.

g. Sew a buttonhole in the other end of the strap (see page 19).

h. Hand sew the button to the opposite top corner of the front (without a strap).

Step 3. Cut and sew waist tie.

a. Cut a 5" × 23½" piece and two 5" × 28" pieces out of fabric B.

b. With *right* sides together, sew all three pieces together along the short sides to create one long strip, with the shortest piece in the middle. Press the seams open.

c. Fold in one long edge lengthwise ½" and press flat. Repeat for the other raw edge.

d. Fold the waist tie in half lengthwise with *wrong* sides together and topstitch along the open and folded edges.

e. Center the waist tie on the apron front and topstitch along each edge to the apron's edges.

f. Fold over each end of the waist tie ¼" then another ¼" and topstitch to finish the edge.

Step 4. Cut out and sew wave bottom edge.

a. Cut a 6" × 28" piece of fabric B. Fold the piece in half lengthwise, *right* sides together.

b. Lay the wave pattern over the folded fabric, matching the straight edge of the pattern to the raw edges of the folded fabric. Use a fabric pencil or fabric marker to trace the wave pattern onto the fabric.

c. Stitch along the traced line.

d. Cut close to the stitched line. Turn right-side-out and press flat.

e. Fold under the raw edge of the wave piece 1¼", then another ¼" and press. Topstitch to secure.

f. Pin the folded edge of the wave piece to the bottom inside of the apron and topstitch in place ¼" from the bottom of the apron.

pocket
MEMO BOARD

fabric

Use 44"-wide, mid- to heavy-weight coordinating cotton prints

Fabric A: ⅓ yard

Fabric B: ⅓ yard

Fabric C: ⅓ yard

Fabric D: ½ yard

½ yard (44"-wide) muslin

3 coordinating fabric remnants

¾ yard (44"-wide) fusible interfacing

other supplies

18" × 24" canvas

Cutting mat

Embroidery floss

Embroidery needle

Fabric pencil

Iron & ironing board

Rotary cutter

Scissors

Sewing machine

Sewing thread in coordinating color

Staple gun and staples

Straight pins

Butterfly templates (on page 122)

PROJECT NOTES

➤ All seams are ¼" unless otherwise stated. (The ¼" seam allowance is included in all of the cutting measurements.)

Step 1. Cut fabric pieces.

a. Cut one 12½" × 12" piece out of each of fabrics A, B and C.

b. Cut a 16½" × 22" piece out of fabric D and the muslin.

c. Cut three 9" × 10" pieces of fusible interfacing.

d. Cut three 3" × 4½" pieces of muslin.

Step 2. Line and sew pockets.

a. Fold under the top edge of fabrics A, B and C ½" and then again another ½" and press flat. Press under what will be the right-hand side of the pocket ¼".

b. Slide a piece of interfacing beneath the top fold of pieces A, B and C (fusible side down) and line up the one side edge of the interfacing to where the fabric has been folded over ¼"; iron the interfacing.

c. Fold under each short side of the small muslin pieces ¼" and press.

d. At the top of each pocket, topstitch ⅜" from the folded edge through all (folded) fabric layers.

e. Fold under both 3" edges of the small muslin pieces 1" to create 1" × 4½" muslin pieces for the labels. Press flat.

f. Machine- or hand-stitch the short edges of each small muslin piece to the front of each pocket, about ½" from the top and centered, as shown.

Step 3. Sew pockets to memo board cover.

a. Fold under one 16" edge of fabric D ½". Line up pocket C about 4½" from the top folded edge and ¼" from the right-hand side edge of fabric D. Stitch a line along the pocket ¼" from the bottom edge to keep it in place on fabric D.

b. Line up pocket B 3" from the top edge of pocket C and sew the bottom edge of the pocket to fabric D.

c. Line up pocket A 3" from the top edge of pocket B and sew the bottom edge of the pocket to fabric D.

d. Fold all pockets into position, pocket C at top, pocket B over pocket C, and pocket A over pocket B. With *right* sides facing, pin 22" edge fabric D to one 22" edge of the large piece of muslin. Sew a ¼" seam. (Note that the side edges of all three pockets are sewn into this seam.)

e. From the front (*right* side), make a row of straight stitches ⅜" on each side of the seamline.

f. Measure over 10" from seamline, joining muslin to fabric D (3d) and mark a vertical line down the left side edges of the pockets. Topstitch over this line.

Step 4. Cut out and appliqué butterflies.

To see this technique demonstrated, see page 23.

a. Create a butterfly stencil (see page 40) from the pattern on page 122. Trace each butterfly onto a different fabric remnant with a fabric pencil.

b. Iron a piece of fusible interfacing behind each butterfly, and then cut out the shape.

c. Pin each butterfly to the large muslin piece and use an appliqué stitch to sew them in place.

d. Thread an embroidery needle with three strands of floss and use a backstitch (page 12) to sew the antennae.

Step 5. Staple fabric to canvas.

a. Line up the fabric where you want it on the canvas. Holding the fabric in place, flip the canvas over. Pull the fabric taut, fold over the raw edges and staple the raw edges into the wood frame of the canvas. Staple once in the center of each side of the wood frame and then continue around the board.

TEMPLATE: FABRIC CARDS

Patterns appear here at full size

Patterns appear here at full size

Patterns appear here at full size

Enlarge image by 200%

TEMPLATE: FABRIC ART

Enlarge image by 200%

TEMPLATE: FLOWER APPLIQUÉ PILLOW

Pattern appears here at full size

TEMPLATE: SPARROW PILLOW

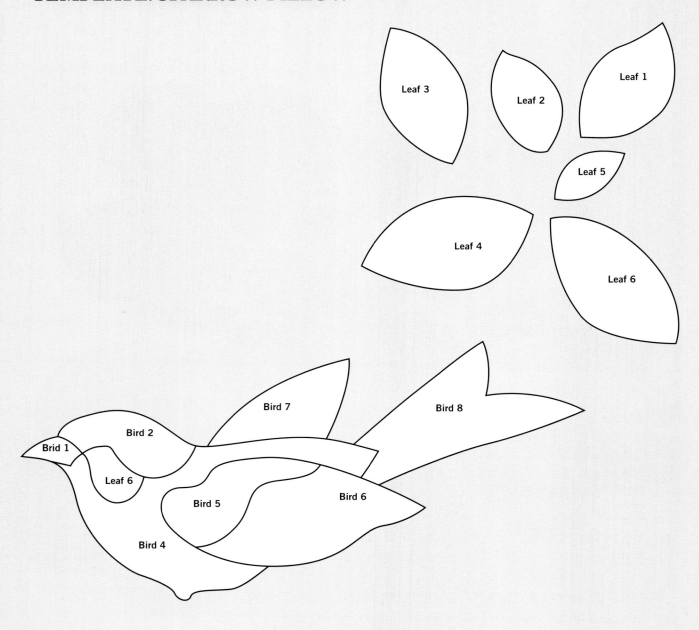

Enlarge image by 200%

Index

sew inspiring!

What's your sewing pleasure?
Thread your needle and sew your next project from one of these fine titles from F+W Media.

Perfectly Fitted
Creating Personalized Patterns
for a Limitless Wardrobe
Lynne Garner

ISBN-13: 978-1-4402-0413-5
ISBN-10: 1-4402-0413-6
paperback • 128 pgs • 9 x 9½ • Z5433

Button and Stitch
Supercute Ways to Use Your Button Stash
Kristen Rask

ISBN-13: 978-1-60061-311-1
ISBN-10: 1-66061-311-X
paperback • 144 pgs • 8 x 8 • Z2913

Free-Style Handmade Bags & Skirts
The Editors at Woonjin Publishing

ISBN-13: 978-1-60061-196-4
ISBN-10: 1-60061-196-6
paperback with pattern insert •144 pgs •
8½ x 11 • Z2795

Jelly Roll Quilts
Pam & Nicky Lintott

978-0-7153-2863-7
0-7153-2863-8
paperback • 128 pgs • 8¼ x 10⅞ • Z2175

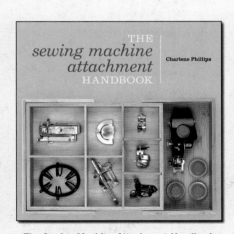

The Sewing Machine Attachment Handbook
Charlene Phillips

ISBN-13: 978-0-89689-923-0
ISBN-10: 0-89689-923-3
paperback • 144 pgs • 8 x 8 • Z3607

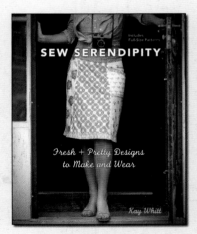

Sew Serendipity
Fresh and Pretty Designs to Make and Wear
Kay Whitt

ISBN 10: 1-4402-0357-1
ISBN 13: 978-1-4402-0357-2
semi-concealed wire-o with box envelope and
patterns 160 pgs • 8 x 10 • Z4958

These and other fine F+W Media titles are available at your local craft retailer, bookstore
or online supplier, or visit our Web site at www.mycraftivitystore.com.